全人教育英语专业本科教材系列

总顾问　刘润清
总主编　文　旭

跨文化思辨阅读教程

（生活篇）

主　编　袁凤识
副主编　秦小雅　李银美
编　者　张翼鸿　高　黎　王亚非
杨仁瑛　赵宏伟　张慧馨
张　潇　徐召华

中国人民大学出版社
·北京·

总 序

英语专业是我国高等外语教育的重要组成部分。高等外语教育责任大、作用大、影响大、意义大，具有工具性、人文性、专业性和国际性的鲜明特点。教材承载着社会价值和文化价值，是人类智慧积累和知识传承的最重要媒介之一，是实现教育目的和功能的最重要手段之一，因而教材的研发和编写已经上升到国家事权的高度。从 2014 年开始，我们组织编写了这套“全人教育英语专业本科教材系列”，目的是推动我国高等外语教育、特别是英语专业教育的发展，更好地满足我国英语专业教育的多元需求。经过编写团队的艰苦努力，本套教材于 2018 年全部出齐，与广大师生见面，其中许多品种已经被评为省部级或者学校级优秀教材。为了适应新形势的飞速发展，迎应我国高等外语教育面临的新机遇和新挑战，锤炼精品，打造品牌，自 2020 年起，我们对本套教材的主干品种进行了全面修订。

一、修订依据

1. 政策依据

“全人教育英语专业本科教材系列”最初编写的政策依据是《国家中长期教育改革和发展规划纲要（2010—2020 年）》、《教育部关于全面提高高等教育质量的若干意见》（教高〔2012〕4 号）以及《外国语言文学类教学质量国家标准》。本次修订，我们认真贯彻《中国教育现代化 2035》、《普通高等学校本科英语类专业教学指南》以及《高等学校课程思政建设指导纲要》等文件的精神，在修订过程中充分考虑到新时代我国英语专业教育的现状，并力求体现当代英语专业教育的本质特征、目标和任务，贯彻为实现目标任务所倡导的外语教育理念、教学原则、教学模式、教学过程、教学方法和教学评价，着力服务并促进我国英语专业教育改革，提升英语专业教育的内涵和质量，更好地提高英语专业学生的英语能力、跨文化交际能力和综合素质，培养全面发展的复合型人才。

2. 理论依据

本套教材编写和修订的理论依据主要是教育学、心理学、语言学、认知神经科学等学科的理论和原则。其教育学依据主要是“素质教育理论”和“全人教育理论”（holistic education），主张“教单科、育全人，教外语、育全人”的外语教育理念；其心理学依据主要是认知心理学、社会心理学和积极心理学中的相关理论，强调英语学习的特殊性，把听、说、读、写、译等基本技能与学生的多元智能有机地结合起来；其语言学依据主要是应用语言学和教育语言学，尤其是终身学习理论下的体验学习、自主学习、合作学习、泛在学习、深度学习以及适应性学习；其认知神经科学依据主要是全脑教育，认知神经科学有助于我们理解人脑的共同之处与个体差异，有助于英语教学的因材施教。人脑和智力具有可塑性，只要学生拥有信心、自尊和动机，外语学习随时都可以成功。

3. 实践依据

教学实践是检验教材质量的唯一标准。在修订过程中，我们充分听取并吸收了所有使用本套教材院校的意见和建议，与一线骨干教师多次召开线上和线下座谈会、研讨会，对于修订教材的指导思想、定位、主干教材的难度和梯度（包括各册之间的有机联系等）、材料取舍、格式体例、练习设计，包括教师用书的编写，都反复推敲、打磨、完善，最后形成共识。我们力求在博采众长、适应新形势、新挑战的基础上，修订出一套能够经得住时间和实践考验的优秀教材。

二、教材特色

在传承初版的基础上，教材的修订进一步强化和突出以下六个方面：

1. 进一步落实立德树人根本任务

习近平总书记指出：“人才培养一定是育人和育才相统一的过程，而育人是本。人无德不立，育人的根本在于立德。这是人才培养的辩证法”（《深入学习习近平关于教育的重要论述》第 49 页）。立德树人是我国教育的根本任务。围绕教育的根本问题“培养什么人、怎样培养人、为谁培养人”，本套教材着力挖掘思政元素，突出中国特色社会主义和中国梦教育、社会主义核心价值观教育、法治教育、劳动教育、心理健康教育以及中华优秀传统文化教育。

2. 继续贯彻“教单科、育全人，教外语、育全人”的全人教育理念

全人教育的理念是“教单科、育全人，教外语、育全人”，倡导人的“终身学习和终身发展”。这一模式体现了人本主义的基本思想：教育和学习就是要把学生培养成为有道德、有知识、有文化、有能力、和谐发展的“完人”。高等外语教育要帮助学生树立正确的世界观、人生观和价值观，教育学生认知、认同和践行社会主义核心价值观。联合国教科文组织和国际教育发展委员会编著的《学会生存：教育世界的今天和明天》就特别强调要“培养完人”（2009: 192），“把一个人在体力、智力、情绪、伦理各方面的因素综合起来，使他成为一个完善的人，这就是对教育基本目的的一个广义的界说”（2009: 195）。

3. 坚持围绕“教育的四大支柱”，突显体验学习、自主学习和深度学习

全人教育特别重视体验学习。本套教材的修订始终立足培养四种基本学习能力，即教育的四大支柱：学会认知（learning to know）、学会做事（learning to do）、学会共同生活（learning to live together）以及学会生存（learning to be），始终把价值塑造融入语言知识、技能和学习策略中，通过任务、活动及练习引导学生进行体验学习、自主学习和深度学习。

4. 加强思辨能力培养

教育的核心任务之一是培养学生的创新能力，创新能力必须以思辨能力为支撑。思辨能力培养一直是欧美高校课程设计的核心，也是全人教育的核心主张之一。本套教材在任务、活动和练习设计中，都以培养学生提出问题、分析问题、解决问题为旨归，引导学生对问题进行批判性思考，并进行有效的输出实践。比如，在修订版《英语国家概况》的练习中，我们就提供了与各章节课文内容相关的原始材料，要求学生在思考、理解的基础上，撰写适当长度的学术作文（论文）。这是培养思辨能力的最有效途径之一。

5. 强调英语的工具性与人文性有机结合

工具性和人文性是一切语言学习包括高等外语教育的本质特征。本套教材的修订除帮助学生掌握英语这一交流和思维工具，提高学生英语听说读写译的能力以及跨文化交际能力之外，还特别强调把以人为本、弘扬人的价值作为设计教材内容的另一核心，精心选取具有丰富人文内涵的素材，使教材以知促行、以行促知，学以致用，并在潜移默化中培育学生的家国情怀。

6. 充分体现文明互鉴和文化交流，培养新时代国际化复合型人才

高等外语教育的国际性体现在文明互鉴和文化交流上，要求培养既具有中国立场、家国情怀，又具有国际化、全球化视野的复合型人才。基于此，本套教材选材严谨、丰富，语言地道、经典，融合中西文化，重视本土问题和国际问题、中西对比等问题，努力培养学生的跨文化意识，提升其跨文化能力。

三、研发团队

本套教材是专家智慧和集体智慧的结晶。顾问是我国著名外语教育专家、北京外国语大学博士生导师刘润清教授，总主编是西南大学博士生导师文旭教授。参加编写的学校主要有（排名不分先后）：西南大学、北京理工大学、华中科技大学、东北大学、内蒙古大学、河南大学、贵州大学、上海海事大学、西南政法大学、山西大学、广州大学、湖南科技大学、华南师范大学、陕西师范大学、西北师范大学、四川师范大学、贵州师范大学、云南师范大学、广西师范大学、海南师范大学、西华师范大学、重庆师范大学、重庆交通大学、重庆理工大学、重庆邮电大学、浙江理工大学、沈阳工业大学、西南石油大学、新疆师范大学、青海师范大学、北京信息科技大学、长江师范学院、中国海洋大学、中国石油大学、济南大学、四川农业大学、长沙理工大学、四川文理学院、河南工业大学等。

在此，我们衷心感谢本套教材的研发团队，衷心感谢本套教材的所有使用院校，衷心感谢中国人民大学出版社对本套教材的长期大力支持。我们会继续虚心听取大家的意见和建议，使本套教材日臻完善。

“全人教育英语专业本科教材系列”编委会
2023 年 4 月

前言

《跨文化思辨阅读教程（生活篇）》将中外文化对比、阅读思辨能力培养、思政元素挖掘等较好地融合在一起，涉及生活方式、旅游景点、价值观、家庭教育、饮食方式、健康、地理、扶贫等方面，具有时新性、前沿性、高阶性的特点。本教材能有效开拓学生的视野，培养学生对中西方生活差异的敏感性和鉴别能力，本教材的阅读和练习，能润物细无声地将课程思政理念传递给学生。

一、教材编写背景

目前，英语专业教材普遍有以下特征：

1. 在英语专业教材中，有跨文化交际教材，有精读和泛读教材，但能将中外文化对比与阅读相结合的教材较为罕见。

2. 跨文化交际教材以英美文化为强势，非英语文化被忽视，中国文化被边缘化甚至失语，从而容易误导教师将跨文化教学等同于以英语目的语文化为主的英美文化教学。因此，有必要在教材中多融入中国文化，讲好中国故事。

3. 精读和泛读教材以语言知识输入和语言技能训练为主，跨文化能力和思辨能力培养处于可有可无的地位，这与《外国语言文学类教学质量国家标准（2018）》"特别突出跨文化能力、思辨能力和创新能力培养"的总体框架相矛盾。

4. 课程思政背景下的思辨阅读教程匮乏。如何在中西文化对比背景下讲好中国故事，挖掘中国的文化传承、历史底蕴、民族团结、诚信友善、家国情怀、爱国主义教育等思政元素，值得深入思考。

本教材正是在这种背景下编写完成的。本教材尝试通过中外英语名家名篇的阅读教学培养学习者的跨文化能力和思辨能力，为英语专业课程思政背景下的思辨阅读教学提供实践参考。

二、教材主要内容

本教材共 8 个单元，供一个学期使用。每单元的阅读材料包括课文背景、课文 A、课文 B 3 个部分，每篇课文后有文本内容练习、语言熟练度练习、观点反思练习等，每单元最后为中外对比练习。

1. 课文背景（Background）

本部分通过 1~2 段文字材料和 / 或 1~2 幅图画，对单元主题进行简短介绍，以便于学生了解单元相关内容，激发学习兴趣。

2. 阅读文本（Text A、Text B）

阅读文本由 Text A 和 Text B 组成，分别对中国文化和外国文化进行介绍。文本多选自英文原版材料或国内权威英文报纸和杂志，语言地道，话题新颖。

3. 文本内容练习（Focus on the Content）

文本内容练习着重考查学生对文章内容的理解能力，包括判断正误、单项选择、回答问题、填表、思维导图等题型，难度递进，引导学生逐渐理解文意。

4. 语言熟练度练习（Increase Language Proficiency）

语言熟练度练习着重提高学生的语言能力，包括释义、填空、词汇扩展、翻译句子、翻译短文等题型，难度递进，旨在帮助学生提高语言基本功。

5. 观点反思练习（Reflect on the Text）

观点反思练习着重培养学生的思辨能力，包括对概念的理解、细节的描述、观点的思辨、思想的表达等阅读题型，难度递进，可提高学生的英语思辨能力。

6. 中外对比练习（Compare and Contrast）

中外对比练习从不同角度启发学生对中外文化差异进行思考，包括中外异同、态度表达等题型，蕴含思政元素，培养学生对中国文化的热爱。

7. 参考译文（Text Translation）

为了帮助读者准确理解文章的意思，尤其是准确理解部分长难句的含义，本教材为所选的文章提供了译文，供学生自学和老师备课时参考使用。

三、教材使用说明

《跨文化思辨阅读教程（生活篇）》可供英语专业一年级及以上学生作为阅读教材使用，也可供非英语专业通过四级的学生作为通识课程教材使用。

教材每单元的练习题都配备了答案，并配有解析说明，开放类题目也有一定的提示，以方便学生查阅参考。

建议在教材使用过程中，教师给学生创造更多的自主学习机会，课前学生可通过预习完成文章阅读和文后练习；课中学生可通过同伴讨论、小组研讨等活动形式，对中外异同对比等深度思考练习发表观点；课后可借助网络资源，完成阅读拓展活动的个人或小组展示，提高信息整合加工能力、团队合作能力、批判性思维能力和创造性思维能力。

由于编者水平有限，难免会有疏漏或不足之处，敬请读者批评指正，以期不断改进和完善。

编者

2023 年 3 月

CONTENTS

目　录

Unit 1

Ways of Life

Background

In this Unit, we will study two passages on ways of life written by Lin Yutang (1895–1976) and Henry David Thoreau (1817–1862).

Text A is an excerpt of "On Going about and Seeing Things", taken from Lin Yutang's *The Importance of Living* (Chapter 11 "The Enjoyment of Travel"). In this book Lin Yutang wisely conveys his opinions on living based on Chinese philosophy. *The Importance of Living* has 14 chapters and discusses mainly two aspects of living, one is about human nature and life philosophy, the other is about 5 approaches on how to enjoy living, including enjoyment of family, nature, travel, culture and basic elements of life.

Text B is an excerpt of "Where I Lived and What I Lived for", Chapter 2 of Henry David Thoreau's masterpiece *Walden*. In 1845, Thoreau went to live alone in a cabin built by himself by Walden Pond, starting his 2-year experiment on Transcendental philosophy. In 1854, the fruit of the experiment was published as *Walden*, an eighteen-chapter long reflection on living simply in nature. In *Walden*, Thoreau, as a philosopher, naturalist and author, artistically expresses his profound understandings on such themes as simplicity, self-reliance, nature, work, spirituality, solitude, etc. *Walden* is now considered to be Thoreau's literary masterpiece for his keen observation on nature, his philosophical speculation, his rich knowledge of Eastern and Western cultures as well as his poetic style. Thoreau's philosophy on simple living in nature has inspired generations of readers worldwide to renew themselves each day.

Text A

On Going about and Seeing Things

By Lin Yutang

1 Travel used to be a pleasure, now it has become an industry. No doubt there are greater facilities for traveling today than a hundred years ago, and governments with their official travel bureaus have exploited the tourist trade with the result that the modern man travels on the whole much more than his grandfather. Nevertheless travel seems to have become a lost art. In order to understand the art of travel, one should first of all be aware of the different types of false travel, which is no travel at all.

2 The first kind of false travel is travel to improve one's mind. This matter of improving one's mind has undoubtedly been overdone. I doubt very much whether one's mind can be so easily improved. Anyway there is very little evidence of it at clubs and lectures. But if we are usually so serious as to be bent upon improving our minds, we should at least during a vacation let the mind lie fallow, and give it a holiday. This false idea of travel has given rise to the institution of tourist guides, the most intolerable chattering kind of interfering busybodies that I can imagine. One cannot pass a square or a bronze statue without his attention being called to the fact that So-and-So was born on April 23, 1792, and died on December 2, 1852. The grown-ups themselves are turned into a group of school children being vociferously lectured to by the guide, and in the case of the travelers of the more studious type, also taking notes very assiduously like good school children.

3 The second kind of false travel is travel for conversation, in order that one may talk about it afterwards. I have seen visitors at Hup'ao of Hangchow, a place famous for its tea and spring water, having their picture taken in the act of lifting tea cups to their lips. To be sure, it is a highly poetic sentiment to show friends a picture of themselves drinking tea at Hup'ao. The danger is that one spends less thought on the actual taste of the tea than on the photograph itself. This sort of thing can become an obsession, especially with travelers provided with cameras, as we so often see on sight-seeing buses in Paris and London. The tourists are so busy with their cameras that they have no time to look at the places themselves. Of course they have the privilege of looking at them in the pictures afterwards when they go home, but it is obvious that pictures of Trafalgar Square or the Champs Elysees can be bought in New York or in Peiping. As these historical places become places to be talked about afterwards instead of places to be looked at, it is natural that the more places one visits, the richer the memory will be, and the more places there will be to talk about. This urge for learning and scholarship therefore impels the tourist to cover as many points as possible in a day, he has in his hand a program of places to visit, and as he comes to a place, he checks it off with a pencil on the program. I suspect such travelers are trying to be efficient even on their holiday.

4 This sort of foolish travel necessarily produces the third type of false travelers, who travel by schedule, knowing beforehand exactly how many hours they are going to spend in Vienna or Budapest. Before such a traveler departs, he makes a perfect schedule for himself and religiously adheres to it. Bound by the clock and run by the calendar as he is at home, he is still bound by the clock and run by the calendar while abroad.

5 In place of these false types of travel, I propose that the true motives of travel are, or

should be, otherwise. In the first place, the true motives of travel should be travel to become lost and unknown. More poetically, we may describe it as travel to forget. Everyone is quite respectable in his home town, no matter what the higher social circles think of him, he is tied by a set of conventions, rules, habits and duties. A banker finds it difficult to be treated just as an ordinary human being at home and to forget that he is a banker, and it seems to me, the real excuse for travel is that he shall be able to find himself in a community in which he is just an ordinary human being. Letters of introduction are all very well for people on business trips, but business trips are by definition outside the category of pure travel. A man stands a poorer chance of discovering himself as a human being if he brings along with him letters of introduction. Against the comforts of being well-received by friends in a foreign country and guided efficiently through the social strata of one's own class, there is the greater excitement of a boy scout in a forest, left to his own devices. He has the chance to prove for himself that he can order a fried chicken with the language of fingers alone, or find his way about town by communicating with a Tokyo policeman. At least, such a traveler can come home with a less tenderfootish dependence upon his chauffeur and butler.

6 A true traveler is always a vagabond, with the joys, temptations and sense of adventure of the vagabond. Either travel is "vagabonding" or it is no travel at all. The essence of travel is to have no duties, no fixed hours, no mail, no inquisitive neighbors, no receiving delegations, and no destination. A good traveler is one who does not know where he is going to, and a perfect traveler does not know where he came from. He does not even know his own name and surname. This point has been emphasized by Tu Lung in his idealized sketch of *the Travels of Minliaotse*. Probably he hasn't got a single friend in a strange land, but as a Chinese nun expressed it, "Not to care for anybody in particular is to care for mankind in general." Having no particular friend is having everybody as one's friend. Loving mankind in general, he mixes with them and goes about observing the charms of people and their customs. This kind of benefit is entirely missed by those travelers on the sight-seeing buses, who stay in the hotel, converse with their fellow passengers from the home country. English travelers in Shanghai make sure that they put up at an English hotel where they can have their bacon and eggs and toast with marmalade at breakfast, and hang about the cocktail lounge and fight shy of any inducement to get them to take a rickshaw ride. They are terribly hygienic, to be sure, but why go to Shanghai at all? Such travelers never allow themselves the time and leisure for entering into the spirit of the people and thus forfeit one of the greatest benefits of traveling. The spirit of vagabondage makes it possible for people taking a vacation to get closer to Nature. Travelers of this kind will therefore insist on going to the

summer resorts where there are the fewest people and one can have some sort of real solitude and communion with Nature.

7 I may suggest that there is a different kind of travel, travel to see nothing and to see nobody, but the squirrels and muskrats and woodchucks and clouds and trees. There is all the difference between seeing things and seeing nothing. Many travelers who see things really see nothing, and many who see nothing see a great deal. We come therefore to the philosophy of travel as consisting of the capacity to see things, which abolishes the distinction between travel to a distant country and going about the fields of an afternoon.

8 The two become the same thing, as Chin Shen'an insisted. The most necessary outfit a traveler has to carry along with him is "a special talent in his breast and a special vision below his eyebrows," as the Chinese dramatic critic expressed it in his famous running comment on the drama *Western Chamber*. The point is whether one has got the heart to feel and the eyes to see. If he hasn't, his visits to the mountains are a pure waste of time and money; on the other hand, if he has got "a special talent in his breast and special vision below his eyebrows," he can get the greatest joy of travel even without going to mountains, by staying at home and watching and going about the field to watch a sailing cloud, or a dog, or a hedge, or a lonely tree.

(From *The Importance of Living*, Chapter 11 "The Enjoyment of Travel")

Focus on the Content

I. Comprehension check.

Write T if the sentence is true, F if it is false.

_________ 1. The development of travel industry has made it possible for people to travel much than before.

_________ 2. Human beings have done too much on trying to improve their mind.

_________ 3. Tourist guides can provide useful information and help tourists enjoy their travel.

_________ 4. When we travel, cameras can help us see things better.

_________ 5. While traveling, one shall try to forget his fame and position, and become an ordinary person.

_________ 6. One of the greatest benefits of traveling is to get to know the spirit of local people.

_________ 7. The farther one travels, the more things one sees.

_________ 8. A good traveler should be able to feel and see.

Ⅱ. Multiple choice.

Choose the best answer to each question.

Gist 1. The whole passage is mainly about ________.

A. how to enjoy the art of travel

B. how to judge false travels

C. how to see less things while traveling

D. how to see more things while traveling

Detail 2. The development of travel is shown in the following aspects except ________.

A. official travel bureaus have expanded tourist industry

B. there are more and better facilities for traveling

C. people travel more than before on the whole

D. people gain more pleasure from travel than before

Detail 3. The three kinds of false travel mentioned in Para. 2–Para. 4 do not include ________.

A. travel to improve one's mind

B. travel to show off in talk

C. travel according to the planned timetable

D. travel to forget

Vocabulary 4. "...and in the case of the travelers of the more studious type, also taking notes very *assiduously* like good school children." The word "*assiduously*" in this sentence might mean ________.

A. diligently　　B. carefully

C. clearly　　D. neatly

Detail 5. When a traveler travels by schedule he will do the following things except ________.

A. know what to see before he starts his travel

B. carry out the travel plan strictly

C. choose interesting places to see after arriving at the place

D. stick to his schedule as he does at home

Inference 6. Lin proposes that if one wants to enjoy the real pleasure of travel, one should ________.

A. try to discover oneself as a human being

B. try to see nothing and nobody

C. try to improve one's ability of feeling and seeing

D. all the above

Rhetoric 7. In the beginning sentence of paragraph 6, ________ is used to emphasize Lin's opinion on a true traveler.

A. a simile

B. a metaphor

C. a symbol

D. a hyperbole

Reference 8. In the first sentence of paragraph 8, "The two become the same thing, as Chin Shen'an insisted.", "the two" refers to ________.

A. seeing things and seeing nothing

B. seeing sceneries and seeing people

C. travel to a distant country and going about the fields of an afternoon

D. travel to a city and travel to nature

Ⅲ. Comprehension questions.

Answer these questions in complete sentences.

1. In Lin Yutang's opinion, what turns travel into a lost art?
2. Why does Lin Yutang say that travel to improve one's mind is a false travel?
3. What's wrong with the second kind of false travel?
4. What's wrong with the third kind of false travel?
5. When we travel to forget, what do we try to forget and what can we gain from this kind of travel?
6. Why does Lin Yutang compare a true traveler to a vagabond?
7. Interpret Lin Yutang's views on good travelers and perfect travelers.
8. What's the difference between travel to see things and travel to see nothing and nobody but nature?
9. In Lin Yutang's opinion, what's the key of the philosophy of travel?
10. According to paragraph 8, how can one enjoy the pleasure of travel? How does Lin Yutang illustrate his point?

Increase Language Proficiency

Ⅰ. Words in context.

Choose the correct definitions for the underlined words.

_______ 1. No doubt there are greater facilities for traveling today than a hundred years ago...

A. abilities B. features

C. conveniences D. places

_______ 2. This false idea of travel has given rise to the institution of tourist guides...

A. organization B. system

C. founding D. custom

_______ 3. This urge for learning and scholarship therefore impels the tourist to cover as many points as possible in a day...

A. forces B. causes

C. leads D. lets

_______ 4. Before such a traveler departs, he makes a perfect schedule for himself and religiously adheres to it.

A. sacredly B. wholeheartedly

C. strictly D. conscientiously

_______ 5. ...he is tied by a set of conventions, rules, habits and duties.

A. conferences B. customs

C. methods D. agreements

_______ 6. Against the comforts of being well-received by friends in a foreign country and guided efficiently through the social strata of one's own class, there is the greater excitement of a boy scout in a forest, left to his own devices.

A. objects B. methods

C. purposes D. aims

_______ 7. The essence of travel is to have no duties, no fixed hours, no mail, no inquisitive neighbors, no receiving delegations, and no destination.

A. interesting B. hating

C. curious D. jealous

_______ 8. Such travelers never allow themselves the time and leisure for entering into the spirit of the people and thus forfeit one of the greatest benefits of traveling.

A. give up B. give in

C. give off D. give back

________ 9. We come therefore to the philosophy of travel as consisting of the capacity to see things, which abolishes the distinction between travel to a distant country and going about the fields of an afternoon.

A. size B. role

C. power D. ability

________ 10. ...they can have their bacon and eggs and toast with marmalade at breakfast, and hang about the cocktail lounge and fight shy of any inducement to get them to take a rickshaw ride.

A. dream B. trend

C. interest D. incentive

Ⅱ. Completion.

Complete the sentences below with the correct form of words from the box.

exploit	bent on	improve	sentiment	bound by
convention	essence	put up	abolish	outfit

1. It is forbidden to ________ outsiders for the night in the dormitory.
2. All new fashion starts out as a reaction against existing ________.
3. She was wearing an expensive new ________.
4. What is being done to stop employers from ________ young people?
5. A rising proportion of the workforce is on short-term or part-time contracts and less ________ old conventions.
6. President Lincoln ________ slavery in the United States.
7. There is no room for ________ in business.
8. An acute observer usually sees the ________ of things at first sight.
9. They are always ________ interfering in other countries' internal affairs.
10. The government aims to ________ public services, especially education.

Ⅲ. Vocabulary expansion: Word forms.

Fill in the table with the correct form of the words and then choose the right word form for each sentence below.

VERB	NOUN	ADJECTIVE	ADVERB
	obsession		
/	sentiment		
		interfering	/
	urge		
depart		/	/
	temptation		

1. We resent foreign ________ in the internal affairs of our country.
2. Students may be ________ to cheat in order to get into top schools.
3. But this trend, and also the sometimes ________ fan culture, is raising concerns.
4. We checked in our luggage and went through to the ________ lounge.
5. He ________ them to set aside minor differences for the sake of peace.
6. The ring wasn't worth very much but it had great ________ value.
7. I think you should try to stop ________ about food if you want to lose weight.
8. There is an ________ need for qualified teachers.
9. I wish my mother would stop ________ and let me make my own decisions.
10. Will they be able to resist the ________ to buy?

Reflect on the Text

Ⅰ. Presentation.

Suppose you were a tourist guide, choose one of the following famous travel resorts in the world mentioned by Lin Yutang in this passage and introduce it to your classmates.

1. Hangchow (City of Hang Zhou)
2. Peiping (Beijing)
3. Trafalgar Square
4. Champs Elysees
5. New York

6. Vienna
7. Budapest

Ⅱ. Debate.

Some travelers think modern photographic equipment is the indispensable outfit of travel, while Lin Yutang regards one's heart and eyes as the most important outfit. What's your opinion? Choose your stance and give your debate for it.

Ⅲ. Point of View.

Make a comment on Lin Yutang's philosophy of travel and its inspiration to us today in the 21st century.

Text B

Where I Lived and What I Lived for

By Henry David Thoreau

1 We must learn to reawaken and keep ourselves awake, not by mechanical aids, but by an infinite expectation of the dawn, which does not forsake us in our soundest sleep. I know of no more encouraging fact than the unquestionable ability of man to elevate his life by a conscious endeavor. It is something to be able to paint a particular picture, or to carve a statue, and so to make a few objects beautiful; but it is far more glorious to carve and paint the very atmosphere and medium through which we look, which morally we can do. To affect the quality of the day, that is the highest of arts. Every man is tasked to make his life, even in its details, worthy of the contemplation of his most elevated and critical hour. If we refused, or rather used up, such paltry information as we get, the oracles would distinctly inform us how this might be done.

2 I went to the woods because I wished to live deliberately, to front only the essential facts of life, and see if I could not learn what it had to teach, and not, when I came to die, discover that I had not lived. I did not wish to live what was not life, living is so dear; nor did I wish to practise resignation, unless it was quite necessary. I wanted to live deep and suck out all the marrow of

life, to live so sturdily and Spartan-like as to put to rout all that was not life, to cut a broad swath and shave close, to drive life into a corner, and reduce it to its lowest terms, and, if it proved to be mean, why then to get the whole and genuine meanness of it, and publish its meanness to the world; or if it were sublime, to know it by experience, and be able to give a true account of it in my next excursion. For most men, it appears to me, are in a strange uncertainty about it, and have somewhat hastily concluded that it is the chief end of man here to "glorify God and enjoy him forever."

3 Still we live meanly, like ants; though the fable tells us that we were long ago changed into men; like pygmies we fight with cranes; it is error upon error, and clout upon clout, and our best virtue has for its occasion a superfluous and evitable wretchedness. Our life is frittered away by detail. An honest man has hardly need to count more than his ten fingers, or in extreme cases he may add his ten toes, and lump the rest. Simplicity, simplicity, simplicity! I say, let your affairs be as two or three, and not a hundred or a thousand; instead of a million count half a dozen, and keep your accounts on your thumb-nail. In the midst of this chopping sea of civilized life, such are the clouds and storms and quicksands and thousand-and-one items to be allowed for, that a man has to live, if he would not founder and go to the bottom and not make his port at all, by dead reckoning, and he must be a great calculator indeed who succeeds. Simplify, simplify. Instead of three meals a day, if it be necessary eat but one; instead of a hundred dishes, five; and reduce other things in proportion. Our life is like a German Confederacy, made up of petty states, with its boundary forever fluctuating, so that even a German cannot tell you how it is bounded at any moment. The nation itself, with all its so-called internal improvements, which, by the way

are all external and superficial, is just such an unwieldy and overgrown establishment, cluttered with furniture and tripped up by its own traps, ruined by luxury and heedless expense, by want of calculation and a worthy aim, as the million households in the land; and the only cure for it, as for them, is in a rigid economy, a stern and more than Spartan simplicity of life and elevation of purpose. It lives too fast. Men think that it is essential that the Nation have commerce, and export ice, and talk through a telegraph, and ride thirty miles an hour, without a doubt, whether they do or not; but whether we should live like baboons or like men, is a little uncertain. If we do not get out sleepers, and forge rails, and devote days and nights to the work, but go to tinkering upon our lives to improve them, who will build railroads? And if railroads are not built, how shall we get to heaven in season? But if we stay at home and mind our business, who will want railroads? We do not ride on the railroad; it rides upon us. Did you ever think what those sleepers are that underlie the railroad? Each one is a man, an Irishman, or a Yankee man. The rails are laid on them, and they are covered with sand, and the cars run smoothly over them. They are sound sleepers, I assure you. And every few years a new lot is laid down and run over; so that, if some have the pleasure of riding on a rail, others have the misfortune to be ridden upon. And when they run over a man that is walking in his sleep, a supernumerary sleeper in the wrong position, and wake him up, they suddenly stop the cars, and make a hue and cry about it, as if this were an exception. I am glad to know that it takes a gang of men for every five miles to keep the sleepers down and level in their beds as it is, for this is a sign that they may sometime get up again.

4 Let us spend one day as deliberately as Nature, and not be thrown off the track by every nutshell and mosquito's wing that falls on the rails. Let us rise early and fast, or breakfast, gently and without perturbation; let company come and let company go, let the bells ring and the children cry—determined to make a day of it. Why should we knock under and go with the stream? Let us not be upset and overwhelmed in that terrible rapid and whirlpool called a dinner, situated in the meridian shallows. Weather this danger and you are safe, for the rest of the way is downhill. With unrelaxed nerves, with morning vigor, sail by it, looking another way, tied to the mast like Ulysses. If the engine whistles, let it whistle till it is hoarse for its pains. If the bell rings, why should we run? We will consider what kind of music they are like. Let us settle ourselves, and work and wedge our feet downward through the mud and slush of opinion, and prejudice, and tradition, and delusion, and appearance, that alluvion which covers the globe, through Paris and London, through New York and Boston and Concord, through Church and State, through poetry and philosophy and religion, till we come to a hard bottom and rocks in place, which we can call reality, and say, This is, and no mistake; and then begin, having a point d'appui, below freshet

and frost and fire, a place where you might found a wall or a state, or set a lamp-post safely, or perhaps a gauge, not a Nilometer, but a Realometer, that future ages might know how deep a freshet of shams and appearances had gathered from time to time. If you stand right fronting and face to face to a fact, you will see the sun glimmer on both its surfaces, as if it were a cimeter, and feel its sweet edge dividing you through the heart and marrow, and so you will happily conclude your mortal career. Be it life or death, we crave only reality. If we are really dying, let us hear the rattle in our throats and feel cold in the extremities; if we are alive, let us go about our business.

5 Time is but the stream I go a-fishing in. I drink at it; but while I drink I see the sandy bottom and detect how shallow it is. Its thin current slides away, but eternity remains. I would drink deeper; fish in the sky, whose bottom is pebbly with stars. I cannot count one. I know not the first letter of the alphabet. I have always been regretting that I was not as wise as the day I was born. The intellect is a cleaver; it discerns and rifts its way into the secret of things. I do not wish to be any busier with my hands than is necessary. My head is hands and feet. I feel all my best faculties concentrated in it. My instinct tells me that my head is an organ for burrowing, as some creatures use their snout and fore paws, and with it I would mine and burrow my way through these hills. I think that the richest vein is somewhere hereabouts; so by the divining-rod and thin rising vapors I judge; and here I will begin to mine. (From Chapter 2, *Walden*)

Focus on the Content

I. Comprehension check.

Write T if the sentence is true, F if it is false.

_________ 1. According to paragraph 1, the highest arts of living is to improve the quality of the day.

_________ 2. From paragraph 1, we can know that Thoreau is confident in our ability to reawaken ourselves.

_________ 3. According to paragraph 2, Thoreau thinks that one can live both meanly and sublimely as long as he lives completely according to his wishes.

_________ 4. According to paragraph 3, our life is mean and wretched because we live like ants and fight like pygmies.

_________ 5. In the opening sentence of paragraph 4, the phrase, “nutshell and mosquito’s wing”, may refer to every obstacle on our journey of life.

________ 6. In paragraph 4, Thoreau coins the word Realometer to refer to the meter that measures how much reality there is, and how deep the freshet of shams and appearances have gathered.

________ 7. In the beginning of paragraph 5, time is compared to a stream to emphasize Thoreau's opinion that life is flowing, shallow, but contains something everlasting.

________ 8. In Thoreau's view, his head is less important than his hands and feet.

Ⅱ. Multiple choice.

Choose the best answer to each question.

Gist 1. The passage is mainly about ________.

A. Thoreau's philosophy of reawakening oneself

B. Thoreau's philosophy of elevating oneself

C. Thoreau's philosophy of living meanly

D. Thoreau's philosophy of living deliberately and simply

Detail 2. According to paragraph 1, the ability to elevate our life can help us in the following aspects except ________.

A. to create artistic works

B. to influence the way we look

C. to affect what we morally do

D. to make right decisions on life

Rhetoric 3. In this sentence from paragraph 2, "I wanted to live deep and suck out all the marrow of life," ________ is used to emphasize Thoreau's opinion on living deliberately.

A. simile

B. metaphor

C. personification

D. irony

Inference 4. In paragraph 3, Thoreau compares our life to a German Confederacy in order to support his idea that ________.

A. our life is made up of too many errors and we should correct them

B. our life is full of unnecessary things and should be simplified

C. our life is immersed in commerce and we should go back to nature

D. our life is too fast and we should slow down

Inference 5. From paragraph 3, we can know Thoreau's attitude towards civilized life is ________.

A. positive

B. negative

C. skeptical

D. supportive

Inference 6. The allusion of Ulysses is used in paragraph 4 to support Thoreau's opinion that ________.

A. we should try to resist temptation like Ulysses

B. we should tie ourselves to the mast like Ulysses

C. we should look another way like Ulysses

D. we should relax our nerves like Ulysses

Grammar 7. In the following sentence from paragraph 4, "Let us settle ourselves, and work and wedge our feet downward through the mud and slush of opinion, and prejudice, and tradition, and delusion, and appearance, *that alluvion* which covers the globe...", *"that alluvion"* is a (an) ________ of "the mud and slush of opinion, and prejudice, and tradition, and delusion, and appearance".

A. attributive

B. predictive

C. appositive

D. adverbial

Inference 8. In paragraph 5, by saying "I know not the first letter of the alphabet", Thoreau means that ________.

A. he is very foolish

B. he is very simple

C. he is eager for more knowledge

D. he is satisfied with his present situation

Ⅲ. Comprehension questions.

Answer these questions in complete sentences.

1. What does the noun phrase, "an infinite expectation of the dawn" mentioned in paragraph 1 refer to?

2. According to paragraph 1, what task does every man have?
3. Interpret your understanding on Thoreau's philosophy of living deliberately mentioned in paragraph 2.
4. According to paragraph 3, what's wrong with our life? And how to solve the problems?
5. What proposals does Thoreau put forward to simplify our life?
6. Interpret the implied meanings of "sound sleepers" mentioned in paragraph 3.
7. What's Thoreau's attitude towards industrial civilization?
8. What figures of speech are mainly used in paragraph 4? Explain their meanings and functions.
9. Please interpret the following two terms mentioned in paragraph 5, "drink shallow" and "drink deeper".
10. According to paragraph 5, what will the author do in the future?

Increase Language Proficiency

I. Words in context.

Choose the correct definitions for the underlined words.

________ 1. ...which does not forsake us in our soundest sleep.

A. wake B. abandon
C. help D. stop

________ 2. I went to the woods because I wished to live deliberately...

A. intentionally B. carefully
C. unhurriedly D. hastily

________ 3. ...to live so sturdily and Spartan-like as to put to rout all that was not life...

A. defeat B. win
C. give up D. get rid of

________ 4. Our life is frittered away by detail.

A. wasted B. saved
C. thrown away D. pushed away

________ 5. The nation itself,...is just such an unwieldy and overgrown establishment, cluttered with furniture and tripped up by its own traps...

A. clashed B. cleaned
C. messed up D. filled up

_________ 6. Let us rise early and fast, or breakfast, gently and without perturbation;...

A. worry

B. fear

C. shame

D. courage

_________ 7. Let us not be upset and overwhelmed in that terrible rapid and whirlpool called a dinner, situated in the meridian shallows.

A. overcome

B. overdone

C. overgrown

D. overtaken

_________ 8. ...and with it I would mine and burrow my way through these hills.

A. cut | B. dig

C. find | D. follow

Ⅱ. Completion.

Complete the sentences below with the correct form of words from the box.

endeavor	genuine	sublime	give an account of	excursion
evitable	forge	upset	glimmer	discern

1. He transforms the most ordinary subject into the _________.
2. We went on an all-day _________ to the Olympic Park.
3. Most patients have basic understanding on medical dispute and think it is _________.
4. To _________ a sword takes great skill.
5. The candles _________ in the corner and she stood by the window.
6. We made an earnest _________ to persuade her.
7. Even the experts took the painting for a _________ Zhang Daqian.
8. He _________ in the novel an air of Sixties nostalgia.
9. We can share our positive attitude with those who are negative or _________.
10. The children failed to _________ what had happened because they were terribly frightened by the murder.

Ⅲ. Vocabulary expansion: Word forms.

Fill in the table with the correct form of the words and then choose the right word form for each sentence below.

VERB	NOUN	ADJECTIVE	ADVERB
elevate			/
	resignation		
fluctuate		/	/
		heedless	
/	commerce		
/	vigor		
/	intellect		

1. But few at the conference in London last week ________ his warning.
2. Beijing has ________ been pushing winter sports into school curriculum.
3. Chess has long been regarded as a measure of ________.
4. High levels of lead could damage the ________ development of children.
5. His career has blossomed and that has given him a certain ________ status.
6. New measures have been adopted to promote local industry and ________.
7. The ________ in the price should be taken into consideration.
8. Pursue those possibilities with ________ and determination, and then watch the good things that will happen.
9. The movie was not a ________ success.
10. Two members ________ from the board in protest.

Reflect on the Text

Ⅰ. Presentation.

In this passage, Henry David Thoreau skillfully uses such figures of speech as simile, metaphor, alliteration, parallelism, repetition, etc. to strengthen his life philosophy. Please choose one figure of speech, pick up the examples from the passage, do research on it and then give your presentation on the usage of the figure of speech. Please include its definition, its meanings and functions in the paragraphs or passage. You can also strengthen your presentation by citing examples from other literary materials.

Ⅱ. Debate.

Some people believe that they should try their best to add something to their life, and this can be called "plus-lifestyle" or "+lifestyle", while others do the opposite, they try to reduce something from their life, and this can be called "minus-lifestyle" or "−lifestyle". Which one do you prefer? Choose your stance and give your debate for it.

Ⅲ. Point of View.

Read the whole chapter of "Where I Lived and What I Lived for", or the whole book of *Walden*, then make a comment on Thoreau's philosophy of simple living in nature and its inspiration to us today in the 21st century.

Compare and Contrast

Ⅰ. Comparison.

Please make a comparison of Lin Yutang and Henry David Thoreau as essayists based on the two passages in this unit.

Ⅱ. Comment.

Please read the whole chapter of "Enjoyment of Travel" and the whole chapter of "Where I Lived and What I Lived for", then make a comment on the influence of Eastern and Western cultures on Lin Yutang and Henry David Thoreau as philosophers and writers.

Unit 2

Collectivism vs. Individualism

Background

Joshua Seong, Verywell

https://www.verywellmind.com/what-are-collectivistic-cultures-2794962

JR Bee, Verywell

https://www.verywellmind.com/what-are-individualistic-cultures-2795273

One of the most widely-recognized distinctions between types of cultures is that between collectivism and individualism. According to *Oxford Languages*, collectivism is "the practice or principle of giving a group priority over each individual in it", while individualism is "the habit or principle of being independent and self-reliant".

Collectivism is a belief system that focuses on collective views, traditions, doctrines, teachings, and practices. A collectivist's sense of self is defined more by who they are with other people, or by their membership in a group. Maintaining social harmony, getting along with others, and meeting social expectations are more important in collectivist cultures. Collectivists tend to communicate in indirect styles—they imply what they really mean, but might say otherwise to avoid conflict or embarrassment. Asian and African cultures tend to be more collectivist, for example.

Individualism is a belief system that focuses on the individual person's development and well-being, rather than on the community or collective development. An individualist's sense of self is defined more by who they are on the "inside," minimizing the influence of factors, contexts, and people "outside" the individual. Individualists tend to communicate in direct styles—they say what they mean, prioritizing that information is conveyed explicitly and unambiguously. European and Western cultures are typically more individualist.

Today, individualism ideologies are mixed with collectivist ideologies everywhere in the world. Just as the world is now viewed as a global village, each and every concept is also global at the moment.

Text A

Collectivism and Its Impact on Contemporary Chinese Society

By Kendra Cherry

1 Collectivist cultures emphasize the needs and goals of the group as a whole over the needs and desires of each individual. In such cultures, relationships with other members of the group and the interconnectedness between people play a central role in each person's identity.

2 Collectivism contrasts with individualism, in which personal needs take precedence. In collectivistic cultures, people are considered "good" if they are generous, helpful, dependable, and attentive to the needs of others. This contrasts with individualistic cultures, which often place a greater emphasis on characteristics such as assertiveness and independence.

3 Common traits of collectivist cultures include:

- Individuals define themselves in relation to others (for example, "I am a member of...").
- Communication is often more indirect to avoid potential conflict or embarrassment.
- Group loyalty is encouraged.
- Decisions are based on what is best for the group.

- Compromise is favored when a decision needs to be made to achieve greater levels of peace.
- Working as a group and supporting others is essential.
- Greater emphasis is placed on common goals than on individual pursuits.
- The rights of families and communities come before those of the individual.

4 Collectivism stresses the importance of the community, while individualism is focused on the rights and concerns of each person. Where unity and selflessness or altruism are valued traits in collectivist cultures, independence and personal identity are promoted in individualistic cultures.

5 These cultural differences are pervasive and can influence many aspects of how society functions. For example, workers who live in a collectivist culture might strive to sacrifice their own happiness for the greater good of the group. Those from individualistic cultures, on the other hand, may feel that their own well-being and goals carry greater weight.

6 While those in individualistic cultures might describe themselves in terms of personality traits and characteristics (e.g., "I am smart, funny, athletic, and kind"), those from collectivist cultures would more likely describe themselves in terms of their social relationships and roles (e.g., "I am a good parent, sibling, and friend").

7 Research shows that collectivist cultures are associated with low relational mobility, a term to describe how many opportunities individuals in a society have to form relationships with people of their choosing. Low relational mobility means that the relationships people have are stable, strong, and long-lasting. These relationships are usually formed due to factors such as family and geographical area, rather than personal choice.

8 In a collectivist culture, it's harder to build relationships with new people, partly because it's generally more difficult to meet them. Strangers are more likely to remain strangers in a

collectivistic culture than they would be in individualistic cultures. Paradoxically, this means that people in individualistic cultures devote more effort and energy toward actively maintaining close relationships, often through increased self-disclosure and greater intimacy.

9 Unlike collectivist cultures where stable relationships are more expected, relationships in individualistic cultures tend to be more fraught and fragile. People must make a greater effort to maintain these relationships. Maintaining harmony within interpersonal relationships is of utmost importance in a collectivistic culture. This is likely because these relationships are extremely difficult to change. Failing to keep the peace can mean long-term unhappiness for everyone involved.

10 Cultural differences also influence the motivation to either stand out or fit in with the rest of the group. Conformity also appears within certain industries. According to research published in the *Journal of Economic Growth*, descendants of pre-industrial agricultural groups tend to favor collectivist cultures, working in more routine occupations as opposed to driving innovation.

11 There are some potential drawbacks of collective cultures. Research shows that collectivistic cultures may foster socially reticent and withdrawn behaviors. People in collectivist cultures tend to be more cautious about sharing their personal problems with their friends. Research shows that they are also cautious when sharing their knowledge within the workplace (even when working in teams), often only doing so if incentivized or if they are highly altruistic. Instead, people often seek out what is known as implicit social support. This involves spending time with supportive people without actually opening up about or addressing the source of the stress.

12 The idea that the group is more important than the individual is very present within the Chinese society. In order to understand the impact of Chinese collectivism on contemporary society, it is important to first examine the history and origins of the concept. Collectivism has long been a part of Chinese culture, with its roots tracing back to the teachings of Confucius in the 5th century BC. According to Confucian philosophy, individuals should strive to uphold the values of harmony, filial piety, and respect for authority.

13 The influence of collectivism can be seen throughout Chinese society today. The concept of collectivism has had a profound impact on economic and social development, as well as on the values and beliefs held by the Chinese people. Collectivism has become deeply entrenched in Chinese culture and continues to shape the way the Chinese people think and act.

14 Confucianism has played a major role in shaping the collective values and beliefs of the Chinese people. Confucianism emphasizes the importance of family and community, and encourages individuals to prioritize the needs of the group over their own. This emphasis on collective values has resulted in a strong sense of loyalty and cohesion among the Chinese people.

15 The concept of collectivism is also closely tied to the traditional Chinese family structure. The family is the cornerstone of Chinese society, and it is considered to be the primary source of support and guidance for individuals. Family members are expected to work together to achieve their goals, and the value of unity is highly emphasized. This focus on collective responsibility has led to a strong sense of belonging and loyalty among family members.

16 Collectivism has had an undeniable impact on economic growth in China. The concept of collectivism has encouraged individuals to work together to achieve common goals, which has resulted in increased productivity and efficiency. Business practices have been greatly influenced by collectivism, with a focus on teamwork and collaboration being essential to success. Furthermore, the emphasis on collective responsibility has enabled entrepreneurs to create successful businesses.

17 Collectivism has also had a positive effect on Chinese entrepreneurship. Entrepreneurs are encouraged to work together to achieve their goals, and the emphasis on collective responsibility has enabled them to create successful businesses. This has allowed China to become one of the world's leading economies, with a thriving entrepreneurial culture.

18 Collectivism has also had a significant impact on social stability in China. The concept of collectivism has encouraged individuals to work together to maintain peace and harmony, and the emphasis on collective responsibility has enabled the government to implement effective policies. Furthermore, the traditional values of Confucianism have helped to foster a sense of unity and solidarity among the Chinese people.

19 The government has also played an important role in promoting social stability. Governmental policies have focused on maintaining order and stability, and have encouraged individuals to work together to achieve common goals. This has resulted in a strong sense of national identity and pride, which has helped to promote social cohesion and stability.

20 It has been demonstrated that collectivism is an important concept that has had a significant impact on Chinese culture. Collectivism has enabled the Chinese people to work together to achieve common goals, and has helped to foster a sense of unity and solidarity among the Chinese people. Collectivism has had a profound impact on Chinese culture, and it continues to shape the values, beliefs, and behavior of the Chinese people.

(Adapted from *What Is a Collectivist Culture?* by Kendra Cherry accessed to at https://www.verywellmind.com/what-are-collectivistic-cultures-2794962#citation-12 and *Is China a Collectivist Culture? Examining the Impact on Contemporary Society* by Happy Sharer accessed to at https://www.lihpao.com/is-china-a-collectivist-culture/)

Focus on the Content

I. Comprehension check.

Write T if the sentence is true, F if it is false, and NI if there is not enough information.

_________ 1. The difference between collectivism and individualism is in what each ideology considers as important: the individual or the group.

_________ 2. The people in an individualist society can easily sacrifice their individual benefits for the sake of the whole society's progress.

_________ 3. Collectivism is a cultural pattern commonly observed among traditional communities like those in Asia, Africa, and Latin America.

_________ 4. Individualism prioritizes group cohesion over individual pursuits while collectivism focuses on human independence and freedom.

_________ 5. "The whole is greater than the sum of its parts" can be used to describe the common ideal of Chinese society.

_________ 6. Collectivism has a great impact on contemporary Chinese society and it has helped China's economic growth and social stability.

_________ 7. Collectivism has enabled China to become one of the world's leading economies, with a thriving entrepreneurial culture.

_________ 8. It is observed that there is an increasing pattern of individualism across the globe and that it is likely associated with a similarly increasing socioeconomic development.

II. Multiple choice.

Choose the best answer to each question.

Gist 1. Which one can best summarize the main idea of the passage?

A. Collectivism is an important concept that has been studied extensively by sociologists and anthropologists.

B. Collectivism refers to a system of shared values, beliefs, and behavior that are held by individuals within a group or society.

C. The passage has explored the concept of collectivism and examined the great impact of collectivism in the context of Chinese culture.

D. One of the most significant aspects of Chinese culture is the major emphasis on collectivism compared to the Western ideal of individualism.

Detail 2. Which one is NOT the valued trait in collectivist cultures?

A. interconnectedness

B. compromise

C. altruism

D. independence

Detail 3. Suppose a foreigner from an individualistic culture is coming to work in a collectivist culture, how will he/she feel about building a close relationship within the new community?

A. easy B. difficult

C. undemanding D. painless

Reference 4. What does "they" refer to in the sentence "Strangers are more likely to remain strangers in a collectivistic culture than they would be in individualistic cultures." in Paragraph 8?

A. strangers B. collectivist cultures

C. people D. individualistic cultures

Vocabulary 5. What does the word "occupations" mean in the sentence "..., descendants of pre-industrial agricultural groups tend to favor collectivist cultures, working in more routine occupations as opposed to driving innovation." in Paragraph 10?

A. jobs

B. regular activities or hobbies

C. situations in which an army or group of people moves into and takes control of a place

D. occasions when someone moves into and starts using a building

Inference 6. Which statement is NOT true according to this passage?

A. While people in collectivist cultures might be more likely to turn to family and friends for support during difficult times, those living in individualist cultures are more likely to go it alone.

B. Chinese societies place more emphasis on collective values and beliefs, in which individuals are viewed as part of a larger collective and are expected to prioritize the needs of the group.

C. Collectivism has enabled the Chinese people to work together to achieve common goals, and has helped to foster a sense of unity and solidarity among the Chinese people.

D. It can be inferred that "I am analytical, sarcastic, and athletic." is said by a person living in collectivist societies but "I am a good husband and loyal friend." is said by a person from an individualistic culture.

Detail 7. Collectivism has had a significant impact on Chinese culture EXCEPT ______.

A. economic development

B. values and beliefs

C. Confucianism

D. social stability

Inference 8. Which one of the following laws is NOT collectivist according to the passage?

A. Labor laws supporting affirmative action or equal opportunity.

B. Laws regarding vaccinations.

C. Healthcare laws.

D. Employment law that a citizen has the right to choose for himself whom he would serve.

Ⅲ. Completion.

Look back at the reading, and complete the chart with the information outlined in the passage.

____1____ of individuals based on their relations to others, ____2____ communication, group ____3____, favor of ____4____, ____5____ on common goals instead of individual pursuits

self-perception in terms of social ____6____ and roles, stable, strong, and ____7____ relationships, ____8____ to the rest of the group

a sense of unity and ____17____ among the Chinese people, a strong sense of national ____18____ and pride

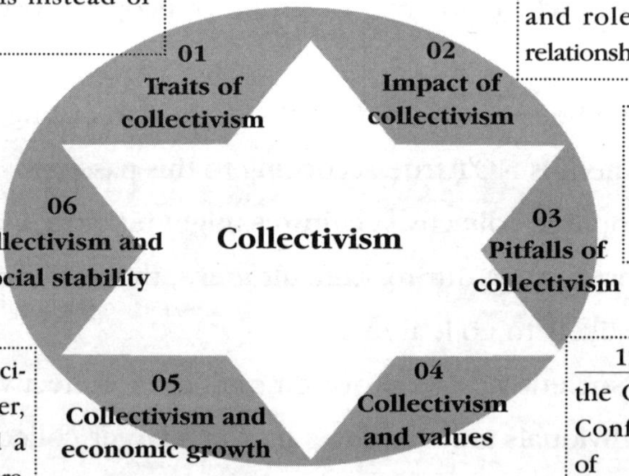

____9____ and withdrawn behaviors, more ____10____ about sharing problems with friends, seeking out ____11____ social support

increased ____15____ and efficiency due to working together, successful businesses and a ____16____ entrepreneurial culture

____12____ values and beliefs of the Chinese people shaped by Confucianism, a strong sense of ____13____ and cohesion, family as the ____14____ of Chinese society

Increase Language Proficiency

I. Words in context.

Choose the correct definitions for the underlined words.

________ 1. ...people are considered "good" if they are generous, helpful, dependable, and attentive to the needs of others.

A. solicitous

B. watchful

C. mindful

D. observant

________ 2. ...workers who live in a collectivist culture might strive to sacrifice their own happiness for the greater good of the group.

A. praiseworthy character

B. something useful or beneficial

C. something that has economic utility or satisfies an economic want

D. something manufactured or produced for sale

________ 3. Unlike collectivist cultures where stable relationships are more expected, relationships in individualistic cultures tend to be more fraught and fragile.

A. filled and weak

B. loaded and easily broken

C. tense and delicate

D. uneasy and vigorous

________ 4. ...individuals should strive to uphold the values of harmony, filial piety, and respect for authority.

A. give support to

B. keep elevated

C. lift up

D. decide on

________ 5. Confucianism emphasizes the importance of family and community, and encourages individuals to prioritize the needs of the group over their own.

A. assign the greatest importance to

B. list something in order

C. rate something in importance

D. treat something in order

______ 6. ...and the emphasis on collective responsibility has enabled the government to implement effective policies.

A. pursue to a conclusion

B. measure

C. provide the instruments for

D. carry out

______ 7. The government has also played an important role in promoting social stability.

A. advancing in station, rank, or honor

B. trying to increase the sales or popularity of one product

C. helping or encouraging something to happen, increase, or spread

D. advancing a student from one grade to the next higher grade

______ 8. Collectivism has had a profound impact on Chinese culture...

A. having intellectual depth and insight

B. very great and intense

C. difficult to fathom or understand

D. extending far below the surface

Ⅱ. Vocabulary expansion: Word forms.

Fill in the table with the correct form of the words and then choose the right word form for each sentence below.

VERB	NOUN	ADJECTIVE	ADVERB
	precedence		
/		generous	
	assertiveness		
define			
/			paradoxically
/	piety		
entrench			/
	collaboration		

1. Value failure for the fact that it shows you _________ what will and will not work.
2. The government worked in close _________ with teachers on the new curriculum.
3. She had to learn that her wishes did not take _________ over other people's needs.
4. There are stories about his _________, the massive amounts of money he gave to charities.
5. Having converted to Buddhism, he promised to be _________.
6. It is a curious _________ that professional comedians often have unhappy personal lives.
7. It's very difficult to change attitudes that have become so deeply _________ over the years.
8. The defendants, who continue to _________ their innocence, are expected to appeal.

Ⅲ. Translation.

Translate the following passage into English.

集体主义有很多优点，包括：

1. 稳定性：集体主义的一个主要优点是，由于社会成员之间的紧密联系，其体系是稳定的。集体主义者的意识形态是“如果你接触其中一个，你就接触了整个群体”。

2. 和平：集体主义环境鼓励所有成员和平共处，他们争论较少，因为所有成员都在携手实现共同目标。集体主义者易对任何阻碍他们共同利益的事情说不。

3. 帮助：很容易得到团队的帮助，因为你的问题变成了每个人的问题。由于每个人都在为社会的利益而共同努力，社会倾向于对其成员的福利负有责任。

4. 效率：国家经济的生产力更高，因为每个人都朝着相同的方向调集自己的资源。更容易启动和完成项目，并开始基础设施的创新。有一个流行的谚语是“人多智广”，我们可以说，对于集体主义来说，这个说法是正确的。

5. 鼓励无私：当实行集体主义时，一个人必须牺牲自己的欲望或愿望。他 / 她这样做是为了他 / 她的国家。反过来，它又教会了个人如何做到无私和以人为本。集体主义者不会做出损害他们兄弟的决定。因此，信任和和谐是维持集体主义社会的基础。

Reflect on the Text

Ⅰ. Presentation.

What do collectivist cultures value? List some examples of collectivist cultures.

Ⅱ. Debate.

Do you agree that China tends to be more collectivist? How do you determine it? Please use some examples in your own life to demonstrate your idea.

Ⅲ. Point of view.

What are some of the traits and challenges that you may encounter if you work or lead a team in a collectivist workplace? How will you overcome the challenges of collectivism?

Text B

Individualism: A Deeply American Philosophy

By Patrick Carroll, Dan Sanchez

1 Individualism is baked into American culture. We value independence, creativity, and self-expression, for example. We admire those who stand out from the crowd for their unique personalities and distinctive talents. We reward high achievers and celebrate heroes.

2 But what exactly is individualism, and how does it fit in the American tradition? Individualism is a philosophy that views people first and foremost as unique individuals rather than as members of a group. It emphasizes the importance of independence, individuality, and autonomy.

3 Many people throughout history, and American history especially, have embodied the spirit of individualism. These people stood out by going where others had not gone before, even when it required an inordinate amount of bravery.

4 Some of the first people in America to embody this spirit were the Western European explorers who settled the New World in the 15th, 16th and 17th centuries. Unlike the vast majority of their countrymen, these explorers were willing to leave their homes and create new lives for themselves in the budding colonies. Of course, life in North America was anything but easy. They faced countless hardships, like disease, cold, and famine. Yet despite all this, the promise of being able to chart their own course propelled them forward. For all its challenges, the New World offered them something that the Old World simply couldn't match: an opportunity to build a new society.

5 By the 18th century, the individualistic ethos of the early explorers had evolved into a fully fledged culture of its own. Then, being more independently minded, the colonists insisted on a significant degree of autonomy from Great Britain. When King George Ⅲ refused to grant them this autonomy, the American Revolution was born, instigated by the *Declaration of Independence*, a veritable individualist manifesto.

6 The Revolution ushered in a new nation: the United States of America. And though the system of government created by the Founding Fathers had many flaws, it was rooted in a philosophy of political individualism, enshrining people's rights to live their lives as they see fit.

7 As the 18th century gave way to the 19th century, a new generation of individualists boldly ventured west into the unexplored territory beyond the frontier. Facing harsh conditions and tremendous uncertainty, these "pioneers" were resolute and resilient, embracing an attitude of self-reliance that came to be known as "rugged individualism."

8 Such self-reliance was explored and celebrated in the works of 19th-century American philosophers like Ralph Waldo Emerson and Henry David Thoreau, who were pivotal figures in the development of individualistic societies.

9 But the history of American individualism hardly stops there. Indeed, as the last reaches of America were being explored, other kinds of explorers, pioneers, and revolutionaries began to emerge, such as inventors and entrepreneurs.

10 One of the most famous entrepreneurs from this time period was Henry Ford. Born in 1863, Ford was an incredibly talented and successful businessman, in large part because of his new and innovative ideas. He revolutionized the automobile industry by introducing assembly lines and mass production, making cars affordable even for the middle and lower classes.

11 But Ford was hardly the only individual making bold changes. Another well-known figure from this time was Thomas Edison, an American inventor and businessman. Famous for inventing the phonograph, the light bulb, and numerous other products, Edison also founded the first investor-owned electric utility company in 1882 in New York City. As with Ford and many other inventors of his time, Edison's curiosity, creativity, and out-of-the-box thinking helped create many of the technologies we now take for granted. Indeed, the willingness to stand out and explore new ideas characterized nearly all of the great inventors of that time, from the Wright brothers to Alexander Graham Bell and countless others.

12 Aside from technology and science, there have been many other individuals who have stood out in cross cultural fields such as arts, athletics, and moral leadership. There was Bob Dylan and John Lennon, Martin Luther King Jr., and Richard Feynman. Though these people had radically different stories and impacts, the one thing they had in common was that they were all uncommon. Indeed, it was their uniqueness, their differentness, their individuality, which caused them to have the influence they did.

13 More recent mold-breakers include Lady Gaga, Johnny Depp, Dave Chapelle, Joe Rogan, Elon Musk, and Steve Jobs. Jobs was not only an individualist himself, but infused individualism into the brand of his company Apple. He especially appealed to people who stood out from the crowd. This approach was famously captured by Apple's 1997–2002 "Think Different" ad campaign, which featured many of the iconic figures mentioned above. The text of the campaign's TV ad says it all.

14 "Here's to the crazy ones, the misfits, the rebels, the troublemakers, the round pegs in the square holes, the ones who see things differently. They're not fond of rules, and they have no respect for the status quo. You can quote them, disagree with them, glorify or vilify them. About the only thing you can't do is ignore them. Because they change things. They push the human race forward. And while some may see them as the crazy ones, we see genius. Because the people who are crazy enough to think they can change the world are the ones who do."

15 From the early settlers to the leaders of today, many individuals have indeed changed the world. But the change they created never came by means of conformity. It always came because of the things that made them stand out.

16 Individualism has had a tremendous impact, not only on culture, but on social theory as well, and political philosophy in particular. The most famous codification of the principles of liberalism is found in the *Declaration of Independence*.

17 "We hold these truths to be self-evident, that all men are created equal, that they are endowed by their Creator with certain unalienable Rights, that among these are Life, Liberty, and the pursuit of Happiness."

18 In framing the *Declaration of Independence*, Thomas Jefferson and his co-authors drew largely on the philosophy of John Locke, who is known as the father of liberalism. In his *Second Treatise of Government*, Locke argued that individual rights are the foundation of a liberal society, beginning with the right of self-ownership. Drawing on this foundation, Locke concluded that it is wrong to violate the property rights of others.

19 "The state of nature has a law of nature to govern it, which obliges every one: and reason, which is that law, teaches all mankind, who will but consult it, that being all equal and independent, no one ought to harm another in his life, health, liberty, or possessions."

20 Governments, Locke said, are instituted by citizens "for the mutual preservation of their lives, liberties and estates, which I call by the general name, property."

21 Regrettably, the transition to treating people as individuals was not as swift as it should have been. Though the ideals espoused in the founding documents of America were noble, the early Americans were reluctant to apply them consistently. Racist and sexist policies in particular were still widespread, and it would take many decades before the laws recognized that women and blacks were just as equal as anyone else. However, with the overthrow of caste systems like slavery, Jim Crow, and the legal subjugation of women, America has come much closer to living up to its individualistic founding principles. And hopefully, this progress can serve as an inspiration for further steps toward the protection of individual rights in the future.

22 Generations of mold-breakers and trailblazers have renewed and improved our world. As time marches forward, new innovators have the opportunity to rise up and make a difference. By resolving to chart our own course, we too can become revitalizing agents of change in a world gone stagnant. We can blaze new trails where others have not gone before, and we can set an example for those who come after us. The opportunity to boldly venture into uncharted territory is more real today than it has ever been. The only question is whether we will seize it. Will you?

(Adapted from *Individualism: A Deeply American Philosophy* by Patrick Carroll & Dan Sanchez accessed to at https://fee.org/resources/individualism-a-deeply-american-philosophy/)

Focus on the Content

I. Comprehension check.

Write T if the sentence is true, F if it is false, and NI if there is not enough information.

_________ 1. Within America's modern day society, people are encouraged to be individuals instead of collectives.

_________ 2. The first people in America to embody the spirit of individualism were the Western European explorers who settled the New World in the 18th century.

_________ 3. Henry Ford, Thomas Edison, Bob Dylan and Steve Jobs are all innovators who led to affordable necessities and luxuries.

_________ 4. America has been faced with a societal conflict which revolves around individualism vs. collectivism.

_________ 5. It is differentness rather than conformity that has made individuals influence the society.

_________ 6. When the Founding Fathers created the *Declaration of Independence*, they had every intention of America maintaining an individualist culture.

_________ 7. Americans were fast in accepting people as individuals because the ideals had been formed ever since the founding documents of America.

_________ 8. The author is doubting whether Americans can seize the chance to change the world.

II. Multiple choice.

Choose the best answer to each question.

Gist 1. What is this reading mainly about?

A. America is faced with a societal conflict between individualism and collectivism.

B. Individualism is a deeply rooted philosophy in America.

C. The natural result of individualism is innovation.

D. Every intention of America is maintaining an individualist culture.

Detail 2. Which one is NOT the example showing that individualism is baked into American culture?

A. Independence, creativity, and self-expression are valued.

B. Unique personalities and distinctive talents are admired.

C. Heroes are easy to be forgotten.

D. High achievers are rewarded.

Inference 3. What nationality is the author of the passage?

A. American

B. Chinese

C. British

D. Not known

Vocabulary 4. What does the phrase "out-of-the-box" mean in the sentence "..., Edison's curiosity, creativity, and out-of-the-box thinking helped create..." in paragraph 11?

A. prefabricated

B. ready to use

C. unusually good

D. innovative

Reference 5. What does "it" refer to in the sentence "The text of the campaign's TV ad says it all." in paragraph 13?

A. ad campaign

B. individualism

C. the company Apple

D. the brand Apple

Detail 6. Which one is NOT mentioned as a field in which many individuals stood out?

A. science and technology

B. arts and athletics

C. moral leadership and politics

D. language and literature

Inference 7. Which is probably the status quo of contemporary America?

A. Racist and sexist policies have been erased.

B. Women and blacks are as equal as anyone else.

C. The legal subjugation of women has been overthrown.

D. The caste systems like slavery haven't been abolished.

Detail 8. Which one is NOT the thing that the new innovators can do?

A. Live in a stagnant world.

B. Rise up and make a difference.

C. Chart their own course.

D. Blaze new trails.

Ⅲ. Completion.

Look back at the reading, and complete the chart with the information outlined in the passage.

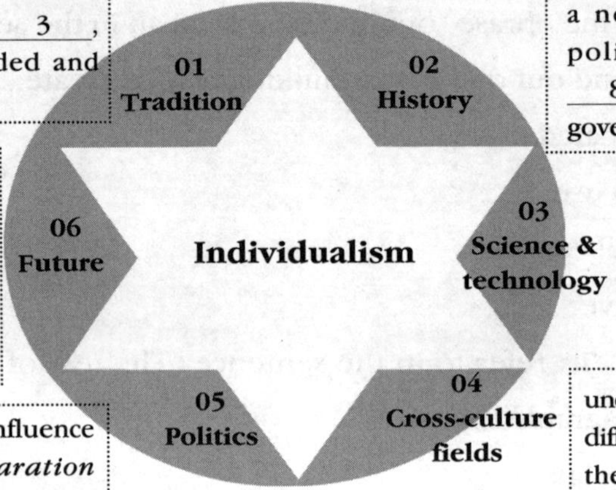

individualism __1__ into American culture, with __2__, creativity, and self-expression valued, unique personalities and distinctive talents __3__, high achievers rewarded and heroes __4__

Western European __5__ creating new lives in North America , __6__ from Great Britain required, a new nation __7__, political individualism __8__ in the system of government

inventors and entrepreneurs __9__, creating new inventions by their curiosity, creativity, and __10__ thinking

uncommon people using __11__, differentness, individuality to make the impact, Steve Jobs being an example who infused __12__ into his brand Apple

owing freedom to the influence of individualism, *Declaration of Independence* as the most famous __13__ of the principles of liberalism claiming that all men are created __14__ and are endowed with certain __15__ Rights

transition was not as __16__ as it should have been, but coming much closer to living up to the __17__ founding principles, more real opportunity to be __18__ in the future

Increase Language Proficiency

Ⅰ. Words in context.

Choose the correct definitions for the underlined words.

______ 1. Individualism is baked into American culture.

A. is made the fixed feature of　　B. is allowed for

C. is added to　　D. is engaged in

______ 2. These people stood out by going where others had not gone before, even when it required an inordinate amount of bravery.

A. unordinary　　B. uncommon

C. excessive　　D. orderly

________ 3. You can quote them, disagree with them, glorify or <u>vilify</u> them.

A. praise

B. spread negative information about

C. elevate the estimation or importance of

D. dignify

________ 4. But the change they created never came by means of <u>conformity</u>.

A. correspondent action

B. action in accordance with some specified standard or authority

C. reforming action

D. concurrent action

________ 5. In <u>framing</u> the *Declaration of Independence*, Thomas Jefferson and his co-authors drew largely on...

A. creating

B. making an enclosing border

C. arranging

D. expressing

________ 6. ...the early Americans were reluctant to apply them <u>consistently</u>.

A. steadily

B. arbitrarily

C. compatibly

D. continuously

________ 7. Generations of mold-breakers and <u>trailblazers</u> have renewed and improved our world.

A. engineers

B. pathfinders

C. creators

D. inventors

________ 8. By <u>resolving</u> to chart our own course, we too can become...

A. making a firm decision

B. finding an answer

C. reaching an agreement

D. bringing an end

Ⅱ. Vocabulary expansion: Word forms.

Fill in the table with the correct form of the words and then choose the right word form for each sentence below.

VERB	NOUN	ADJECTIVE	ADVERB
	creativity		
/	autonomy		
		veritable	
			radically
	inspiration		
		revitalizing	/
		stagnant	
venture			/

1. The new president has made some ________ changes to the company.
2. ________ water is not flowing, and therefore often smells unpleasant and is dirty.
3. The four stages of ________ thought are preparation, incubation, illumination and verification.
4. Few Europeans who had ________ beyond the Himalayas had returned to tell the tale.
5. Congress has tried dozens of approaches to ________ decaying urban and rural areas.
6. Broadcasting, television, cinema, books, newspapers and magazines in ________ areas use one or several local languages.
7. Both poets drew their ________ from the countryside.
8. This method is reasonable and quite satisfactory in the preliminary experimental ________.

Ⅲ. Translation.

Translate the following article into English.

个人主义有一些优点，包括：

1. 赞美多样性：个人主义文化存在的前提是每个人都是独一无二的，因此生活在个人主义群体中的人更有可能意识到并公开支持思想、背景、经验、外貌等的多样性。

2. 鼓励自我表达：由于个人主义文化鼓励个人对意义及重要性有强烈的自我概念，他们鼓励人们表达自己的情绪、信念和想法。

3. 注重个人发展：个人主义文化认为，每个人都可以（也应该）在一生中成长和进步，从而形成一个鼓励和强化个人成就和发展的群体。在这些文化中，个人往往更加独立，对自己无须外力辅助的自立能力更加自信。

Reflect on the Text

Ⅰ. Presentation.

What do individualist cultures value? List some examples of individualist cultures.

Ⅱ. Debate.

Do you agree that America tends to be more individualistic? How do you determine it? Please use some examples that you can find in the books or on the Internet to demonstrate your idea.

Ⅲ. Point of view.

What are some of the traits and challenges that you may encounter if you work or lead a team in an individualist workplace? How will you overcome the challenges of individualism?

Compare and Contrast

Ⅰ. Presentation.

Read the following two quotes and analyze what cultures they emphasize. What are the differences between the two cultures?

"Favourable weather is less important than advantageous terrain, and advantageous terrain is less important than unity among the people."—Mengzi

"If a man does not keep pace with his companions, perhaps it is because he hears a different drummer. Let him step to the music which he hears, however measured or far away."—Henry David Thoreau

Ⅱ. Comment.

Which work environment do you prefer to work in, the individualist culture that prioritizes the needs of the individual or the collectivist culture that prioritizes the needs of the group? Give your reasons to justify your choice.

Unit 3

Parenting

Background

Education has been universally recognized as a key factor in people's growth and development. Naturally, parents across the world put it as the top concern in their childrearing practice. However, parenting styles differ greatly at both individual and cultural levels. Such differences, on the one hand, give parents opportunities to learn from each other and from other cultures, and on the other hand, add to their anxiety as to how to raise their children and how to be a parent. When learning from the parenting styles of other cultures, parents may encounter cultural stereotypes or the trap of blind imitation. At the individual level, however, examples of tiger moms or overprotective parents have caused much heated debate. It is simply not easy to find a suitable parenting style.

The two texts in this unit give us a glimpse of the concerns of Chinese and American parents and the problems they are faced with. Chinese parents have changed their parenting styles over the past few decades due to profound social changes. American parents, on the other hand, are cautioned against the potential harms of overprotective parenting. The insightful discussions in the texts could also help us understand the tough situations parents have to cope with, such as the society's changing demands for children, the increasing anxiety about the prospect of their children due to competition in the job market, the mismatch between the goals of family education and school education, and the pressure on parents from popular cultural beliefs, or even from certain policies.

Text A

What Is a "Good Child"?—Raising Child in Changing China

By Jing Xu

[1] In 2011, Yale law professor Amy Chua published her memoir *Battle Hymn of the Tiger Mother*, and so-called Asian parenting styles—involving ferocious discipline, frequent shaming, and even corporal punishment, all in the single-minded pursuit of academic success—were a hot topic in mainstream American media.

[2] Unsurprisingly, Chua's book was quickly translated into Chinese—but with an interesting twist. In place of Chua's original eye-catching title, the Chinese edition was entitled simply *Mothering in the United States*. Even more surprising was the memoir's icy reception across the Pacific. Many Chinese mothers who had read the book said that Chua's parenting style didn't resonate with their experiences at all. If anything, they found the "tiger mother" approach rather depressing, if not outright bizarre.

[3] The "tiger mother" archetype capitalized on and reinforced certain long-held stereotypes

about Chinese people in the West, but many of these stereotypes are long out of date. How has this change taken place? What does it mean to be a good child in 21st-century China? And what, if not strict obedience, do today's Chinese parents want from their kids?

4 Back in the early 1990s, when the anthropologist David Y.H. Wu surveyed Shanghai families about their parenting practices, he found that raising obedient children was still the paramount priority. A good child was an obedient child, something Wu attributed to a mix of influences. On the one hand, he saw parents' focus on discipline as a response to widespread concern at the prospect of a generation of "spoiled" only children. On the other, he saw in it the influence of what he called China's "authoritarian, collective, and nationalistic" culture.

5 Two decades later, however, there appeared a very different parenting landscape. When asked what moral traits they valued most in their children, 41% of parents said "sociableness," followed by "kindness and caring" and "independence." "Obedience" was the least popular choice: just 2% of parents said it was the most important trait for their children to learn.

6 These results hint at a changing conception of what it means to be a good child in China. Although concern about spoiled singleton children never went away, strict disciplinary solutions—known in academic circles as "authoritarian parenting"—have fallen out of favor in the country. Instead, since the early 2010s, Chinese parents have sought to instill in their kids good social behaviors and a sense of independence.

7 This process shouldn't be understood as a linear development towards so-called Western, individualistic parenting styles. It is true that "Western" childrearing approaches have been re-packaged and sold to urban middle-class consumers as authoritative and scientific. It is also true that these texts, with their emphasis on children's autonomy and socio-emotional intelligence, have shaped Chinese parenting values. But Chinese parents do not blindly absorb or follow Western models. They deliberately evaluate these ideas and compare them against their own circumstances.

8 Chinese parents' aspiration to cultivate more sociable children, for example, didn't just arise from a desire to mimic Western parenting styles; it is at least partly the product of declining faith in academic performance as the sole determinant of their kids' future. In recent years, as competition in schools and on the job market has grown fiercer, many Chinese have come to believe that academic credentials are no longer enough to distinguish job candidates, and interpersonal skills are increasingly seen as an important indicator of a child's future success.

9 The desire to cultivate greater independence, meanwhile, is related to the same fears of spoiled only children that once led parents down the disciplinarian road. In particular, many young parents expressed anxiety that their children were too sheltered, and that their inner

psyches had become too vulnerable. Independence thus took on new meaning: not a sign of disobedience, but of self-reliance and psychological resilience. This resilience is particularly prized given the fierce competition and challenging road parents see facing the next generation.

10 Yet, if parents' understanding of what makes a good child is changing, many schools' definitions of what makes a good student remain stuck in the past. Young parents looking to nurture their children's independence or preserve their creativity often have to compromise their ideals in the face of an approach to education that still prioritizes conformity and obedience.

11 For instance, one mother expressed her concern at the preschool's penchant for putting on tightly choreographed performances. Her three-year-old son's class had spent a month rehearsing their dance routine for the Children's Day holiday. "They're children, not athletes," she complained. "I would like to see them doing things naturally and spontaneously, and I think that might be more beautiful than an impeccable collective dance where every child has to move in the exact ways their teacher told them to. It's like a robot show".

12 The school system is not the only harsh reality facing today's parents. Many parents found it particularly hard to cultivate morality in their children in a broader social environment that still attaches great importance to winning at all costs. Parents cherished the ideal that children should be innocent and pure, expressing their "natural" goodness and kindness without being polluted by the hypocrisy and artifice of the adult world. Yet they also feared that innocent, genuinely kind children wouldn't be fit for the real society that awaits them.

13 That reality helps explain a seemingly contradictory phenomenon: While Chinese parents may individually reject the "tiger mother" approach, they have spent the past decade signing their kids up for evermore intense workloads and tutoring classes. In the most extreme case, a 5-year-old attended eight extracurricular classes on a single weekend. But the motivation for this arms race isn't necessarily intrinsic. Rather, many parents feel forced to push their children, even as they worry that raising a good kid isn't always the same as raising a good student. Rather than resorting to convenient cultural stereotypes, we need to understand how Chinese people navigate the dilemmas and challenges in the world's most competitive educational environment.

14 Anxieties regarding what it means to raise a "good" child in today's China are quite common whether you're in a major metropolis or rural county seat. Chinese parents rarely want to think of themselves as authoritarian "tiger mothers," but they also know that the real world is no place for sheltered kittens.

(Adapted from an essay of the same title by Jing Xu accessed to at https://blog.westminster.ac.uk/contemporarychina/what-is-a-good-child-raising-children-in-a-changing-china/)

Focus on the Content

I. Comprehension check.

Write T if the sentence is true, F if it is false.

_______ 1. Amy Chua's parenting style aroused a lot of public attention in the United States.

_______ 2. Chinese parents are eager to learn from the tiger mom.

_______ 3. Ferocious discipline, frequent shaming, and corporal punishment are typical features of the Chinese parenting style.

_______ 4. Chinese parents loved to raise obedient children in the 1990s.

_______ 5. Today's Chinese parents care more about their children's sociableness than obedience.

_______ 6. Chinese parents regard Western parenting approaches as scientific and authoritative.

_______ 7. In China, strict disciplinary solutions have been considered necessary to keep singleton children from being spoiled.

_______ 8. Many Chinese schools still emphasize obedience and conformity.

_______ 9. Chinese parents view independence as a sign of self-reliance and psychological resilience.

_______ 10. Many Chinese parents push their children hard because the social environment attaches great importance to winning at all costs.

II. Multiple choice.

Choose the best answer to each question.

Detail 1. What is Chinese readers' reception of *Battle Hymn of the Tiger Mother* like?

A. It's warmly welcomed.

B. It is sharply criticized.

C. It doesn't make much stir.

D. It triggers heated debate.

Inference 2. Which of the following is NOT a feature of stereotyped Chinese parenting style?

A. Caring and loving.

B. Authoritarian.

C. Harsh.

D. Disciplinary.

Detail 3. What drove Chinese parents to put obedience as a top priority when raising children according to Wu's study?

A. The expectations from their culture and the fear for their children's future.

B. The lessons taken from Western models.

C. Their aspirations to cultivate more sociable children.

D. The conventions of the society.

Detail 4. In China, what used to be regarded as the sole determinant of children's future?

A. Children's social-economical intelligence.

B. Children's IQ.

C. Children's good behavior.

D. Children's academic performance.

Inference 5. According to the author, Chinese parents' attitude toward Western parenting approaches is ________.

A. negative B. conservative

C. critical D. casual

Detail 6. According to a recent survey, which of the following moral traits is valued most by Chinese parents?

A. Independence.

B. Kindness.

C. Sociableness.

D. Caring.

Detail 7. Which of the following might NOT be regarded as an indicator of a child's future success?

A. Academic performance.

B. Interpersonal skills.

C. Independence.

D. Innocence.

Inference 8. In a challenging and competitive environment, what quality is particularly prized?

A. Psychological resilience.

B. Kindness.

C. Goodness.

D. Obedience.

Inference 9. What causes Chinese parents' anxiety in childrearing today?

A. The pressure from other parents.

B. The disparity between the ideal and the reality.

C. The differences between the Chinese model and the Western model.

D. The requirements from school.

Inference 10. How should today's Chinese parents treat their children according to this article?

A. They should follow the example of the tiger mom.

B. They should neither be too harsh nor too protective to their children.

C. They should push their children hard.

D. They should shelter their children from the hypocrisy and artifice of the adult world.

Ⅲ. Comprehension questions.

Answer the following questions based on what you have read in the text.

1. What is the stereotyped Chinese parenting style in the West?
2. How did many Chinese parents respond to the tiger mom's parenting style? Why?
3. Why isn't the idea of obedience as popular with Chinese parents as before?
4. What does it mean to be a good child in 21st-century China?
5. Why do Chinese parents often compromise their ideals in the face of school?
6. Why do Chinese parents push their children?

Increase Language Proficiency

Ⅰ. Words in context.

Choose the word or phrase that is closest in meaning to the underlined word or phrase in the sentence.

________ 1. The tiger mother's parenting style involves <u>ferocious</u> discipline, frequent shaming, and even corporal punishment.

A. intense B. strong

C. frightful D. strict

______ 2. The original eye-catching title is replaced with a simple one.

A. interesting B. sharp

C. extraordinary D. exciting

______ 3. The "tiger mother" archetype capitalized on and reinforced certain long-held stereotypes about Chinese people in the West.

A. focused on B. drew on

C. was related to D. referred to

______ 4. ...he found that raising obedient children was still the paramount priority.

A. task B. precedence

C. concern D. superiority

______ 5. There is widespread concern at the prospect of a generation of "spoiled" only children.

A. future B. expectation

C. likelihood D. prediction

______ 6. When asked what moral traits they valued most in their children, 41% of parents said "sociableness".

A. trails B. characters

C. values D. rules

______ 7. ...strict disciplinary solutions—known in academic circles as "authoritarian parenting"—have fallen out of favor in the country.

A. cruel B. tyrannical

C. domineering D. powerful

______ 8. They deliberately evaluate these ideas and compare them against their own circumstances.

A. access B. calculate

C. consider D. weigh

______ 9. ...many schools' definitions of what makes a good student remain stuck in the past.

A. unmovable B. intact

C. unchanged D. old-fashioned

______ 10. But the motivation for this arms race isn't necessarily intrinsic.

A. plan B. decision

C. desire D. practice

II. Completion.

Complete the sentences below with the correct form of words from the box.

intrinsic	reinforce	aspiration	priority	single-minded
rehearse	impeccable	contradictory	nurture	discipline
depressing	authoritative	compromise	stereotype	obedient

1. She is very ________ about her career.
2. Strict ________ is imposed on army recruits.
3. He has ________ to fame and greatness.
4. Financial security was high on his list of ________.
5. He doesn't conform to the usual ________ of the businessman with a dark suit and briefcase.
6. He was always ________ to his father's wishes.
7. Children ________ by loving parents can grow more healthily.
8. Education has its ________ value in terms of abstract concepts like intellect, wisdom, and knowledge.
9. The climate of political confusion has only ________ the country's economic decline.
10. Yesterday's unemployment figures were as ________ as those of the previous 22 months.
11. She had ________ taste in clothes.
12. I'm looking for an ________ book on this subject to prove my theory.
13. I refuse to ________ my principles.
14. We are faced with two apparently ________ statements. I wonder which one we could believe.
15. We were given only two weeks to ________ the new play.

III. Vocabulary expansion: Collocations.

Fill in the blanks with proper nouns, verbs, adjectives, or prepositions to complete the collocations in the following sentences according to the text. Change the form when necessary.

1. ________ punishment is the infliction of physical pain upon a person's body as punishment for a crime or infraction.
2. They felt obliged to resort ________ violence to solve their problems.
3. He was sweating from the ________ heat.

4. They told him a disastrous world trade war must be avoided ________ all costs.
5. The rebels seem to be trying to capitalize ________ the public's discontent with the government.
6. ________ competition in the market forces them to seek lower wages.
7. The visit helped to focus world attention ________ the plight of the refugees.
8. The concept of kindness should resonate ________ your spiritual beliefs.
9. He did something contradictory ________ his orders.
10. The regulations were ________ date and confusing.
11. Her parenting style has been a ________ topic in mainstream American media.
12. These parents aspire to ________ more independent children that can fit for the competitive society.
13. Such dressing style has ________ out of favor.
14. Kindness, integrity, courage, and honesty are important moral ________ prized by the family.
15. Strict ________ is necessary for military training.

Ⅳ. Translation.

Translate the following passage into English.

心理学家将育儿定义为“把孩子从婴儿期抚养到成年的过程”。孩子从一出生，就完全依赖父母来满足他们当前的生理需求，而且依赖父母满足他们的精神、智力和社会需求。如果这些需求得不到满足，儿童的成长和发展就会受到阻碍，而忽视这些需求则会对儿童的身心发展产生持久的负面影响。因此，对孩子的培育是孩子生活中不可或缺的一部分。

Reflect on the Text

Ⅰ. Analyze.

1. What are the main arguments in this text?
2. How does the author present these arguments?

Ⅱ. Debate.

Parents all want to cultivate good children. But what is a “good child”? Give your own definition of a “good child” and develop a debate on what moral traits of children should be more cherished.

III. Comment.

Give your comment on the different parenting styles mentioned in this text.

Text B

Overprotective Parents and a New Generation of American Children

By Ryan Chae

1 The past decade witnessed a growing trend in America: overprotectiveness. More specifically, a growing overprotectiveness by Americans toward American children that is being reflected in policy-making and legal decisions, and that has left older generations shaking their heads. Generational gap notwithstanding, mounting evidence and research have begun to reveal a disturbing effect of this trend that should be cause for real concern. Overprotective parents, and the norms that prevail from an overprotective attitude toward children, are threatening to build a generation of young Americans that are highly risk-averse, fearful, and unprepared to become engaged citizens and active leaders.

2 Overprotective parenting describes a collection of behaviors by parents toward their children that work together in an attempt to prevent children from taking on any risks to their emotional or physical health. Sheltering, constant supervision and micromanagement, prevention

of taking responsibility, excessive catering and over-consoling, controlling of the social sphere, and excessive caution are all identifiable behaviors that can be considered a part of the scheme of overprotective parenting. Many people will find most of these behaviors, if not all, to be very familiar simply because they have become more commonplace in today's dialogue and observable in our own personal lives.

3 As for why this trend is occurring, there are several concurrent trends that not only support the conclusion that overprotective tendencies are on the rise, but also help us understand the bigger picture of where we may be headed.

A Deteriorating Sense of Trust

4 Americans do not trust one another as much anymore. An analysis based on data compiled by the General Social Survey (GSS) from 1972 to 2012, illustrates how the percentage of Americans who said that most people can be trusted dropped from about 46% in 1972 to about 32% in 2012. Separating by generation, the data also shows significant drops in trust from Baby Boomers to Millennials. Forty to fifty percent of people within the "older generations" demographic believed that most people can be trusted, while only 25 percent of Generation X individuals and only 19 percent of Millennials answered yes to the same question.

5 Part of this difference could be due to the various generations being in different stages of their lives, but the difference is significant enough to show that this loss of trust correlates with the increase in overprotectiveness among parents. When Americans begin to trust one another less, and in particular the Millennials who are now parents, they begin to place more restraints on their children and supervise them more for fear of others influencing their children. They do not let their children roam around their neighborhood, and they control their children's interactions with other kids and adults.

Technology

6 Technological advancements of the past decade have contributed vastly to the changes we see in parenting. No longer do parents send their children outside when they are bored, rather parents now opt for giving their children electronic devices to keep them entertained. Whether this change is a good or bad one is not within the scope of the issue of overprotective parents, but it does illustrate how easy it has become for parents to be overprotective. In the age of GPS tracking and smartphones, keeping tabs on your children every minute of the day has become easy, and not contacting your kids for hours is more difficult.

The Media and Interconnectedness

7 Why have many people pointed to the media when asked why parents have become more overprotective? The answer: greater interconnectedness. As a result of technology, greater interconnectedness seems to be the root of why some parents try to protect their children from danger. Being able to access news and information from across the nation, it is easy to fall into a trap of believing that what happens on the other side of the nation can just as easily happen in your place. It breeds an illusion of constant danger and risk that does more harm than good.

Higher Parenting Expectations

8 The final concurrent trend relevant to this discussion is the idea that there has been a cultural shift in parenting expectations. Parents are often encouraged nowadays to be more protective of their children and more in control of their education and future. When science and progress seem to be solving all the problems and risks associated with the human condition, why can't parents take the same scientific approach to parenting and control the environment in which they nurture their children to provide them with a safe and happy life? To a growing number of parents, it is not inconceivable at all. It is necessary and morally justifiable.

Effects of Overprotection

9 All these concurrent trends combine to form this image of how and why today's style of parenting, relative to that of previous generations, is unique in its degree of overprotectiveness. But what does overprotective parenting mean?

10 Some would argue that today's parenting has created better parents, more successful children, and helped parents be more present in their children's lives. Thus, instead of a trend toward overprotectiveness, some would argue that it is more accurate to describe this trend as a trend toward better parent-child relationships.

11 However, the research and data prove otherwise. Despite some parents' best intentions, technology and other contributing factors make it easy for parents to be too present in their children's lives and to intervene and exercise control over their children's lives when they so choose. The ease at which parents can do these things makes it all the more frequent in occurrence.

12 As for the effect of overprotection on the well-being of the child, studies have shown that overprotective parenting can lead to risk aversion, a dependency on the parents, a higher risk of psychological disorders, a lack of strong coping mechanisms, and chronic anxiety. A child

that is not allowed to take risks or make his or her own choices is bound to face a lot of anxiety and trouble when having to face the harsh realities of a chaotic world. Interestingly enough, the effects of overprotectiveness share uncanny similarities to those of neglect, albeit to a lesser degree.

13 All in all, children become less equipped to deal with the stressors of the world as adults. College students have higher rates of severe mental illness and higher rates of students on psychiatric medicine than those of only a decade ago, and interviews with several hundred professionals at campus counseling centers reveal that "a lack of coping skills is precisely what distinguishes today's college students." Younger generations today are generally more likely to rank their stress levels above that of older generations as well. Part of the reason for these differences can be attributed to the youth not having learned how to deal with stress as well as older individuals have, but part of it can also be attributed to children being sent off to college without the necessary self-management skills that are learned through independent thought and risk-taking earlier on in their lives.

14 As a nation, we have to ask ourselves what kind of people we want to be. A people that rely on their parents and their nation to provide for them, or a people that contribute to the good of those around them. The way we parent and are parented is oftentimes a reflection of how we perceive the world and how we act as citizens. To have overprotectiveness become a hallmark of American parenting is to progress toward a society of people that asks for more than it gives. Parents should have more faith in the ability of their children to overcome, to take risks, and to be independent. Only then may we be able to reinvigorate the optimism and spirit that this nation seems to have lost and sorely needs today.

(Adapted from an essay of the same title by Ryan Chae accessed to at https://bpr.berkeley.edu/2019/4/16)

Focus on the Content

I. Comprehension check.

Write T if the sentence is true, F if it is false.

________ 1. Overprotectiveness has become a growing trend among American parents.

________ 2. Children with overprotective parents tend to shun risks.

________ 3. Overprotective parents respect their children and encourage them to take responsibility.

_________ 4. The older generations of Americans show a higher level of trust in others.

_________ 5. The loss of trust is caused by overprotectiveness in parenting style.

_________ 6. Technological advancements make it more convenient for parents to keep track of their children.

_________ 7. Media information can make parents more open-minded in raising their children.

_________ 8. Parents can provide their children with a safer and happier life now.

_________ 9. Overprotectiveness helps build a better parent-child relationship.

_________ 10. Parents' overprotection does more harm to their children than good.

II. Multiple choice.

Choose the best answer to each question.

Inference 1. What is the older generations' attitude towards overprotective parenting?

A. Supportive.

B. Disapproving.

C. Indifferent.

D. Worried.

Inference 2. Which of the following is an indicator of overprotective parenting?

A. Love.

B. Care.

C. Constant supervision.

D. Frequent shaming

Detail 3. Which of the following generations have the lowest level of trust in others?

A. The Babyboomers.

B. The Millennials.

C. The Generation X.

D. The Beat Generation

Detail 4. About the relationship between distrust and overprotectiveness, which of the following statements is true?

A. There is no relationship between the two.

B. Distrust can lead to parents' overprotective behavior.

C. Overprotection is the cause of distrust.

D. Overprotection and distrust occur at the same time.

Detail 5. What is the role of technology in the development of the overprotective parenting style?

A. Technology makes it easier for parents to be overprotective.

B. Technology makes it possible for parents to be overprotective.

C. Technology quickens the development of parents' overprotection of their children.

D. Technology makes parents more willing to be overprotective.

Inference 6. What can be inferred from Para. 7 about American media?

A. American media often report danger and risks.

B. American media often offer parenting tips.

C. American media strengthen the interconnectedness of American society.

D. American media often exaggerate danger and risks.

Detail 7. Which of the following is NOT an effect of overprotection on the well-being of children?

A. Risk-aversion.

B. Higher risk of psychological disorder.

C. Dependency on the parents.

D. A lack of communicative skills.

Inference 8. What can be inferred from Para. 12?

A. Neglect is another trend on the rise.

B. Neglect also does great harm to children's well-being.

C. Overprotection may turn into neglect.

D. Overprotection is equal to neglect.

Prediction 9. What may happen as a result of children's lack of self-management skills?

A. They will experience more stress.

B. They will find it difficult to finish their college study.

C. They will rely more on psychiatric medicine.

D. They will not know how to deal with the stressors of the world.

Detail 10. What is the author's advice to parents?

A. They should reinvigorate optimism.

B. They should give their children more trust.

C. They should reform their parenting style.

D. They should realize their responsibility to the nation.

Ⅲ. Comprehension questions.

Answer these questions in complete sentences.

1. What is the current situation of overprotective parenting in the United States?
2. What's the definition of overprotectiveness?
3. What factors contribute to the rise of overprotective parenting?
4. What's the author's general attitude towards technology?
5. What harm can overprotective parenting do to children?

Increase Language Proficiency

Ⅰ. Words in context.

Choose the word or phrase that is closest in meaning to the underlined word or phrase in the sentence.

1. ...mounting evidence and research have begun to reveal a disturbing effect of this trend.

A. increasing B. stunning
C. enough D. solid

2. They are unprepared to become engaged citizens and active leaders.

A. busy B. interested
C. committed D. involved

3. These are all identifiable behaviors of overprotective parenting.

A. identical B. remarkable
C. obvious D. recognizable

4. Americans are having a deteriorating sense of trust.

A. worse B. declining
C. eroding D. poor

5. American parents now begin to place more restraints on their children.

A. pressure B. control
C. limit D. concern

6. Technological advancements of the past decade have contributed vastly to the changes we see in parenting.

A. devoted B. attributed
C. led D. given rise

7. It breeds an illusion of constant danger and risk that does more harm than good.

A. creates B. offers

C. casts D. cultivates

8. To a growing number of parents, this parenting style is not inconceivable at all.

A. unheard of B. incredulous

C. unbelievable D. unimaginable

9. Overprotective parents often intervene and exercise control over their children's lives.

A. interrupt B. interfere with

C. intercede D. involve

10. To have overprotectiveness become a hallmark of American parenting is to progress toward a society of people that asks for more than it gives.

A. sample B. center

C. feature D. mark

II. Completion.

Complete the sentences below with the following expressions in their proper forms.

advancement	excessive	supervise	illusion	deteriorate
reinvigorate	intention	commonplace	correlate	attribute

1. She ________ her success to hard work and a little luck.
2. I felt ________ after a rest and a shower.
3. I did it with the best (of) ________, but I only succeeded in annoying them.
4. He could no longer distinguish between ________ and reality.
5. A high-fat diet ________ with a greater risk of heart disease.
6. A team was sent to ________ the elections in Nicaragua.
7. There are good opportunities for ________ if you have the right skills.
8. Long queues are ________ in front of some popular museums.
9. There are fears that the situation might ________ into full-scale war.
10. There was a period of ________ warmth which melted some of the polar ice.

Ⅲ. Translation.

Translate the following passage into Chinese.

By loading kids with high expectations and micromanaging their lives at every turn, parents aren't actually helping. At least, that's how Julie Lythcott-Haims sees it. With passion and wry humor, the former Dean of Freshmen at Stanford makes the case for parents to stop defining their children's success via grades and test scores. Instead, she says, they should focus on providing the oldest idea of all: unconditional love.

Reflect on the Text

Ⅰ. Analysis.

Analyze the structure of the text and draw a thinking map for it.

Ⅱ. Debate.

Debate on the pros and cons of overprotective parenting.

Compare and Contrast

Discussion.

Compare and contrast the parenting problems Chinese parents and American parents are faced with. What similarities and differences do they have?

Unit 4

Poverty and Wealth

Background

China has made remarkable achievements in poverty alleviation in the past 70 years since the founding of the People's Republic of China. According to statistics released by the World Bank, over the past 40 years, the number of people in China living below the international poverty line has dropped by more than 850 million—this represents 70 percent of the total world figure. With the highest number of people moving out of poverty, China was the first developing country to realize the UN Millennium Development Goal for poverty reduction.

As it was reported in 2020 in America, the path toward economic recovery in the U.S. has become sharply divided, with wealthier Americans earning and saving at record levels while the poorest struggle to pay their bills and put food on the table. The Pew Research Center crunched the numbers and revealed that upper-income families have almost seven times as much wealth as middle-income families and 70 times as much wealth as lower-income families. Pew found that 46% of American families fall into the middle tier, while about 33% are lower-income families. The remaining 21% are upper-income families.

Text A

China Creates a World Miracle in Poverty Reduction

By Cong Peiwu

1 Before I came to Canada for my posting in 2019, many friends recommended Arxan to me, which is a small city in the foothills of Greater Khingan Range in north China. They told me that the scenery there was as beautiful as that of Banff in Canadian Rockies and was quite worth a visit. It is a pity that I was unable to make a trip due to a tight schedule.

2 After I arrived in Canada, I looked up some materials about Arxan out of curiosity and found this small city was indeed unusual with beautiful lakes, forests and snowcapped mountains, as well as vast grasslands and the largest group of hot springs in the world. Unlike Banff, Arxan had remained a key national-level poverty-stricken county by 2011. There was no adequate food or clothing for locals, let alone any tourism industry. Thanks to the national strategy of poverty alleviation through tourism development, the tourism industry in Arxan was promoted, helping the poor people blaze a trail full of hope featuring "tourism plus poverty alleviation". The tourism

revenue of Arxan reached 5.27 billion yuan (about $813.16 million) in 2018, increasing by 280 percent compared to 2013. In 2019, Arxan was officially removed from the list of national-level poverty-stricken counties.

3 Arxan is merely an epitome of the miraculous poverty alleviation of China. Over the past 70 years, the Chinese government has lifted 850 million people out of poverty. During the four decades of reform and opening-up alone, 750 million people have been lifted out of poverty. Since the 18th National Congress of the Communist Party of China, the Chinese government has given top priority to the battle against poverty in its governance and organized the world's biggest and toughest poverty-relief battle in human history. Since 2012, an average of more than ten million people, equivalent to the population of a medium-sized European country, had been lifted out of poverty each year. In November 2020, China accomplished its poverty alleviation target of the new era on schedule, with all 832 poor counties removed from poverty, eradicating absolute poverty and overall regional poverty, and achieving the poverty reduction target of the UN 2030 Agenda for Sustainable Development 10 years ahead of schedule.

4 China takes "targeted poverty alleviation" as a basic strategy, which is also a key feature of its poverty alleviation effort. The poverty alleviation plans are tailored to different groups of people, which include increasing production, relocating the poor, ecological compensation, strengthening education, improving social security, etc. China has also introduced a list of top 10 poverty alleviation projects such as poverty alleviation through e-commerce, tourism, and photovoltaic power generation projects. With such policies, China's poverty elimination actions have benefited a wide range of Chinese people including minorities. By the end of 2019, over 2.92 million people in northwest China's Xinjiang Uygur Autonomous Region have shaken off poverty. In Tibet Autonomous Region in southwest China, all 74 poor counties have been removed from the poverty list, and the net income per year per capita increased from 1,499 yuan at the end of 2015 to 9,328 yuan in 2019, which means eliminating absolute poverty in history for the first time. In Guangxi Zhuang Autonomous Region in southwest China, a provincial-level region with the largest population of minorities in China, all the 54 poor counties have been removed from the poverty list, and all the people of the Zhuang ethnic group have been lifted from poverty.

5 China has made great contributions to the world poverty alleviation process. China has the highest number of people moving out of poverty worldwide, accounting for over 70 percent of the global poverty alleviation effort. Besides, it established the China-UN Peace and Development Fund, South-South Cooperation Assistance Fund, and made solid progress in cooperation

projects under such frameworks as the Pilot Project of Poverty Reduction Cooperation in East Asia and the China-Africa Poverty Reduction and People's Welfare Plan. China has helped establish 24 agricultural technology demonstration centers in Africa, benefiting more than 500,000 local people.

6 Poverty eradication is a challenge for all and the top priority of the 2030 Agenda for Sustainable Development. According to the United Nations Development Programme (UNDP), the world population living in extreme poverty will exceed 1 billion by 2030 due to the COVID-19. Thus, realizing global poverty eradication is still an ongoing battle. China and Canada have a lot to share in eradicating poverty, promoting gender equality and tackling climate change. It is our common aspiration to pursue a better life. Let's join hands to make greater contributions to world poverty alleviation and strive for a better future for mankind.

(http://ca.china-embassy.gov.cn/xw/202102/t20210209_10321240.htm)

Focus on the Content

I. Comprehension check.

Write T if the sentence is true, F if it is false, and NI if there is not enough information.

________ 1. I visited Arxan for the first time in 2019.

________ 2. After I looked up the materials about Arxan, I was attracted by the beauty of nature and went to visit Mount Arxan.

________ 3. The tourism industry in Arxan was promoted, helping the poor people build railways.

________ 4. The battle against poverty the Chinese government organized is the world's biggest and toughest poverty-relief battle in human history.

________ 5. It took the Chinese government about 8 years to achieve the success of poverty alleviation after the 18th National Congress of the CPC.

________ 6. In Tibet Autonomous Region, the net income per year per capita grew by 9,328 yuan in 2019 compared with that in 2015.

II. Multiple choice.

Choose the best answer to each question.

Detail 1. I looked up some materials to know more about Arxan because ________.

A. I planned to work there

B. I planned to live there

C. I was curious about the city it is located in

D. I was curious about its scenery

Detail 2. Which is **NOT** the beautiful scenery of Arxan?

A. The beautiful lakes, forests and mountains.

B. The vast grasslands.

C. The great waterfalls.

D. The largest group of hot springs.

Detail 3. When was Arxan officially removed from the list of national-level poverty-stricken counties?

A. In 2011. B. In 2013.

C. In 2018. D. In 2019.

Detail 4. Until the end of 2020, China has accomplished its poverty alleviation target of the new era in the following aspects except ________.

A. an average of more than ten million people has been lifted out of poverty each year since 2012

B. all poor counties were removed from poverty

C. absolute poverty and overall regional poverty across the country was eradicated

D. the poverty reduction target of the UN 2030 Agenda for Sustainable Development was achieved as scheduled

Vocabulary 5. The poverty alleviation plans are <u>tailored</u> to different groups of people. (Para. 4) What is the meaning of the underlined word?

A. planned according to the schedule

B. made fit for a specific purpose

C. designed as required

D. finished on schedule

Inference 6. What is the author's attitude towards the cooperation of China and Canada?

A. Positive.

B. Negative.

C. Indifferent.

D. Worried.

Inference 7. This article may be published in ________.

A. a story book

B. a scientific journal

C. a history book

D. a newspaper

Ⅲ. Comprehension questions.

Answer these questions in complete sentences.

1. What contributes to the tourism development of Arxan?
2. What percentage of tourism revenue in 2018 was increased in Arxan compared with 2013?
3. What is the key feature of Chinese poverty alleviation effort?
4. What are the poverty alleviation plans in detail in China?
5. How many poverty alleviation projects have been implemented in China?
6. What contributions has China made to the world poverty alleviation process?
7. What has hindered the achievement of the global poverty reduction goal in recent years?

Increase Language Proficiency

Ⅰ. Words in context.

Complete each sentence with the correct answer.

1. If a member of an armed force gets a **posting** to a particular place, they are sent to live and work there for a ________ period.

A. limited B. unlimited

2. If something is **adequate**, it is ________ to be used or accepted.

A. good enough

B. not good enough

3. If one amount or value is the **equivalent** of another, they are ________.

   A. similar   B. the same

4. If someone said something with **absolute** certainty, he was ________ certain about it.

   A. completely   B. partly

5. To **demonstrate** a fact means to make it ________ to people.

   A. true   B. clear

6. A **pilot** project is one which is used to ________ before deciding whether to introduce it on a larger scale.

   A. test an idea   B. promote products

7. If a city is regarded as the **epitome** of the country, it should be the ________ of the country.

   A. center   B. typical example

8. If you give **priority** to something or someone, you treat them as ________ than anything or anyone else.

   A. more important   B. more careful

II. Completion.

Complete the sentences below with the correct form of words from the box.

miracle	eradicate	remain	autonomous
ethnic	range	ecology	strive

1. The film begins with an aerial view of the great mountain ________ of Alps.
2. He is seen as having made a significant contribution towards the ________ of corruption.
3. He believes only theoretical science can create ________.
4. She ________ to read the name on the stone pillar in darkness.
5. It ________ true that sport is about competing well, not winning.
6. The change of coffee planting mode endangers the very existence of certain animals and birds, and even disturbs the world ________ balance.
7. He treated us as ________ individuals who had to learn to make up our own minds about important issues.
8. All Singaporeans have to pass exams in the official language of their ________ group as well as English.

Ⅲ. Vocabulary expansion: Word forms.

Fill in the table with the correct form of the words and then choose the right word form for each sentence below.

VERB	NOUN	ADJECTIVE	ADVERB
	recommendation	/	/
sustain			
		accomplished	/
	/		exceedingly
		aspirational	
secure		secure	
alleviate		/	/
		compensatory	/

1. She failed to _________ the task because she was in poor health.
2. The group was considered to be a risk to national _________.
3. The organization works to _________ world hunger and disease.
4. I had the operation on the _________ of my doctor.
5. Environmental _________ is the key strategy against the backdrop of the growth of human population and the rampant exploitation of environment by humans.
6. If you do not _________ to excellence, you will never achieve it.
7. Women who are the victims of intentional discrimination will be able to get _________.
8. The child has skipped to the third grade as he did _________ well in his studies.

Reflect on the Text

Ⅰ. Presentation.

Sum up the achievements of "targeted poverty alleviation" strategy of the Chinese government.

Ⅱ. Debate.

Which is more important, knowledge poverty alleviation or economic poverty alleviation?

Ⅲ. Point of View.

How much do you know about the contributions of China in the achievement of poverty reduction?

Text B

A Million New Millionaires Were Created in the US Last Year, and the Richest Got Richer, Report Says

By Robert Frank

A man sits on the Wall Street bull near the New York Stock Exchange (NYSE) on November 24, 2020 in New York City.

1 The roaring stock market and crypto gains created more than a million new millionaires in the US last year, according to a new report.

2 The number of Americans with $1 million or more in investible assets surged to a record 14.6 million in 2021, up from 13.3 million in 2020, according to a report from wealth research firm the Spectrem Group.

3 The growth rate of over 10% was the strongest in years, boosted by trillions of dollars in wealth created by the stock market, crypto and other assets.

4 "It was the strongest year ever for millionaire creation in all segments," said George Walper, president of Spectrem Group.

5 The wealth surge was strongest at the top. The number of Americans worth $25 million or more surged by 18%. There are now a record 252,000 Americans worth $25 million or more, up from 214,000 in 2020. By contrast, the number of so-called "mass affluent" investors—or those with between $100,000 and $1 million—grew by about 2%.

6 The stock market was by far the largest engine of wealth creation for millionaires and the wealthy in 2021. The S&P 500 gained 27% last year, while the Nasdaq was up 21%. The wealthiest 1% of Americans gained over $3 trillion in stock-market wealth in 2021, according to Federal Reserve data.

7 Crypto and other assets—such as NFTs, collectibles and real estate—also gained in value, adding to the wealth of the wealthy. The total market cap of crypto assets, despite wild swings in prices, gained $1.5 trillion last year to over $2.3 trillion, according to CoinGecko.

8 Values of private-equity and venture-capital investments also surged. Since the wealthy can afford to put more of their money in investments, especially those with the highest risks and rewards, ultra-millionaires benefitted more than the mass affluent in 2021.

9 "The wealthy have the greatest exposure to the broadest investments," Walper said. "It wasn't just traditional liquid markets that did well last year. It was also alternative investments, real-estate investments and crypto."

10 The wealth gains at the top also widened the wealth gap in the US. The share of wealth held by the top 1% grew to a record 32% last year, according to the Fed.

11 Wealth experts say it's unlikely that last year's gains will be sustained in 2022, given soaring inflation, rising interest rates and a potential economic slowdown. Stock market declines have already started trimming the paper fortunes of investors. The Nasdaq is down 14.5% for the year, while the S&P is down 8.4%.

12 "Every day changes, so it's hard to predict where the year will wind up," Walper said. "But the first few months of 2022 have already painted a different picture than 2021."

13 The combined fortune of 26 of the world's richest people is equal to the total wealth of the 3.8 billion poorest people. This startling disparity in wealth is according to a report from the charity Oxfam. It reported that since the global financial crisis in 2008, the number of billionaires in the world has doubled. They are also getting $2.5 billion richer every day. This is in stark contrast to the world's less fortunate—the poorest half of the planet is seeing its wealth slowly shrink as prices of commodities increase, wages are squeezed and land prices and rents

rise. Oxfam's report highlights the growing gap between the world's rich and poor and the ever-widening gap in wealth inequality.

14 The report says that most of the world's mega-wealthy have made their huge fortunes from technology companies like Amazon, Microsoft and Facebook. The world's richest person is Amazon founder and CEO Jeff Bezos. His amassed $100 billion fortune is 100 times greater than the annual health budget of Ethiopia. Oxfam said it was time to try and redress the imbalance in wealth. It recommended taxing income at fairer levels, increasing tax on personal earnings and corporate profits, and eliminating tax avoidance schemes commonly used by companies and the super-rich. It said, "In many countries, a decent education or quality healthcare has become a luxury only the rich can afford."

(Adapted from https://www.cnbc.com/2022/03/17/million-new-millionaires-were-created-in-us-last-year-report-says.html and https://breakingnewsenglish.com/1901/190123-wealth-inequality.html)

Focus on the Content

I. Comprehension check.

Write T if the sentence is true, F if it is false, and NI if there is not enough information.

_________ 1. The stock market and crypto gains have created more than a million millionaires in the US in the past years.

_________ 2. From 2020 to 2021, the number of Americans with $1 million or more in investible assets surged by more than 10%.

_________ 3. According to George Walper, in 2022, millionaires in all fields increased the most.

_________ 4. The S&P 500 Index increased 6% higher than the Nasdaq Index in 2021.

_________ 5. The wealthiest 1% of Americans gained nearly $3 trillion in stock-market wealth in 2021.

_________ 6. In 2021, the American untral-millionaires benefitted more than the mass affluent because of the investments of the highest risks and rewards.

_________ 7. The rich have more access to a wide range of investments, including liquid markets, alternative investments, real estate investments and crypto.

_________ 8. The wealth experts are very optimistic about the economic situation in 2022.

Ⅱ. Matching.

For the following items, match each item in Column I with an appropriate item in Column II. Use each letter only once.

I	II
1. NFT (Non-fungible Token)	A. U.S. central bank system responsible for monetary policy
2. Fed (the Federal Reserve system)	B. the person with the highest rank in a business company
3. S&P (Standard&Poor's) 500 index	C. cryptographic assets on a blockchain with unique identification codes and metadata
4. CoinGecko	D. property in the form of land and buildings, rather than personal possessions
5. Nasdaq	E. a crypto currency market data platform used for tracking the crypto market
6. real estate	F. things considered to be worth collecting (not necessarily valuable or antique)
7. collectables	G. a computer system in the US that supplies the current price of shares to the people who sell them
8. CEO (Chief executive officer)	H. a market-capitalization-weighted index of the 500 largest U.S. publicly traded companies

Ⅲ. Comprehension questions.

Answer these questions in complete sentences.

1. Compared with 2020, what is the increase in the number of Americans with investable assets of more than one million dollars in 2021?
2. What contributed to the 10% growth rate of the American wealth with $1 million in investible assets?
3. Which group has the fastest growth in wealth in the past two years?
4. By 2022, what is the number of Americans with more than 25 million dollars?
5. According to the Federal Reserve, what was the largest engine of wealth creation for millionaires in 2021?
6. What has widened the gap between rich and poor in the United States?
7. What did Walper mean by "But the first few months of 2022 have already painted a different

picture than 2021."?

8. What are Oxfam's suggestions on redressing the wealth imbalance?

Increase Language Proficiency

Ⅰ. Words in context.

Complete each sentence with the correct answer.

1. **Crypto assets** are a ________ representation of value that you can transfer, store, or trade electronically.

   A. digital　　B. entity

2. If you **venture** to do something, it requires ________.

   A. efforts　　B. courage

3. If an organization **trims** something such as a plan or policy, they reduce it ________ in extent or size.

   A. slightly　　B. sharply

4. If two things are in **stark** contrast to one another, they are ________.

   A. very different from each other　　B. the same to each other

5. If scientists **amassed** data, they ________ data.

   A. accumulated　　B. studied

6. If you **profit** from something, you gain some ________ from it.

   A. support　　B. advantage

7. A **luxury** is something ________ which is not necessary but which gives you pleasure.

   A. expensive　　B. giant

8. The **charity** aims to provide ________ to people in need.

   A. mercy　　B. assistance

Ⅱ. Completion.

Complete the sentences below with the correct form of words from the box.

potential	asset	sustain	soar
crisis	segment	alternative	disparity

1. Her ________ include shares in the company and a house in France.
2. A sentence can be divided up into meaningful ________.
3. He has ________ his fierce social conscience from young adulthood through old age.
4. We try to help all students realize their full ________.
5. One of her priorities will be to eliminate pay ________ between men and women for equal work.
6. The ________ had a negative effect on trade.
7. Shenzhou-12 manned spaceship ________ into the air on June 17, 2021.
8. The company has decided not to use static routing for the four routers inside the company. They found an ________ solution.

Ⅲ. Vocabulary expansion: Word forms.

Fill in the table with the correct form of the words and then choose the right word form for each sentence below.

VERB	NOUN	ADJECTIVE	ADVERB
predict			
		investible	/
/	affluence		
/			privately
inflate			/
		exposed	/
	startler		
/			decently

1. He ________ his life savings in his daughter's business.
2. The level of ________ is a serious impediment to economic recovery.
3. It's a fallacy that the ________ give relatively more to charity than the less prosperous.
4. There is a need for more resources so that all children may have a ________ education.
5. It began to appear as if this were not so ________ necessary to maintain her present state.
6. Workers at the nuclear plant were ________ to high doses of radiation.
7. Beds can be screened off to give patients more ________.
8. Skilled readers make use of context and ________.

Reflect on the Text

Ⅰ. Presentation.

Please list the ways the rich people in the United States accumulate wealth.

Ⅱ. Debate.

Is it immoral for the rich not to help the poor?

Ⅲ. Point of View.

How do you evaluate the fact that the rich Americans are getting richer and the poor ones are getting poorer?

Compare and Contrast

Ⅰ. Presentation.

Read the following passages and analyze the difference between poverty alleviation in China and the United States. What are the differences in the treatment of the poor under the policies of the two countries?

Passage 1

Common prosperity is the fundamental principle of socialism with Chinese characteristics. It refers to a state in which the whole nation enjoys ample food and clothing through hard work and mutual help. China is a vast country with a large population. Achieving common prosperity does not mean that all will become prosperous at the same time, but that, where conditions permit, some areas and some people may develop faster than others, and they will then help those that lag behind to catch up, so that all become prosperous over time. China will adhere to the basic socialist economic system and income distribution system, adjust the pattern of national income distribution, step up efforts to adjust secondary distribution and work hard to narrow income gaps so that everyone can share in more of the fruits of development fairly, and move steadily toward common prosperity.

(http://guoqing.china.com.cn/keywords/2017-06/20/content_41063580.htm)

Passage 2

Seattle City Council is considering a new criminal code regulation that would see it become the first municipality in the US to excuse misdemeanor crimes if they can be linked to poverty, addiction, or mental health disorders. The concept, known as the poverty defense, was discussed Tuesday by the Seattle City Council's Public Safety Committee after it was introduced by Council member Lisa Herbold and Anita Khandelwal, the King County's director of the Department of Public Defense. Under the defense, an accused suspect could possibly be absolved of a crime—such as theft, assault, or trespassing—if they committed the offense to meet a basic need to survive. "In a situation where you took that sandwich because you were hungry and you were trying to meet your basic need of satisfying your hunger; we as the community will know that we should not punish that. That conduct is excused," Khandelwal said, according to KOMO. The proposal, however, excludes misdemeanors related to domestic violence and impaired driving. Khandelwal also suggested the creation of a public fund for restitution, to compensate theft victims even if the offender cannot pay them. While the proposed legislation hasn't even yet been written, it is generating a lot of discussion between local lawmakers.

(https://www.amren.com/news/2020/12/seattle-city-council-considers-new-poverty-defense-to-excuse-misdemeanor-crimes/)

Ⅱ. Debate.

Do you think realizing common prosperity should be the essential requirements of the society?

Unit 5

Philosophy

Background

Great minds love wisdom. Back to the 5th century BCE, East or West, a bunch of great thinkers devoted themselves to pursuing truth and knowledge, among whom Confucius and Socrates were noticeably well-known. This unit is designed to give some insights into the two great figures. They both live by principles and strive for truth; however, their exploration and findings obviously differ a lot.

Confucius, born in 551 BCE, is regarded as one of the greatest thinkers in China and his wisdom was recorded in the *Analects*, which has a far-reaching and crucial influence on the future generations. Karyn L. Lai, Professor of Philosophy in the School of Humanities and Languages at University of New South Wales, guides us on how to read the ancient classics, the *Analects*. Ten years later after the death of Confucius, a well-known figure in Athens was born—he was Socrates. Impressively, in 399 BCE, at the age of 70, Socrates was condemned to death for "not worshipping the gods" and "corrupting the young." The second text is excerpted from the last part of the famous dialogue, "The Apology of Socrates," recorded by Plato. To this day, his eloquent words about death seem to still echo in our ears.

Text A

Confucius and *The Analects*

By Karyn L. Lai

1 Troubled by the unrest of the Spring and Autumn period, Confucius (Kongzi) (551 BCE–479 BCE) proposed the ethical reform of society. His proposal involved the elimination of the power abuse and exploitative behaviors of those in power. The process was to be initiated and led by leaders of society who were the role models of broad education and ethical insight. As the advocate of these ideas, Confucius is often recognized as the founder of the Ru-jia doctrine (School of Literati), which is called the Confucian tradition in the West. The Ru-ists were educated men who sought to share and realize their insights on the ethical administration of government. Historically, the Ru-ists were part of a larger movement of educated scholar-officials (shi) appointed as advisers to those in power. Ru-ist education consisted in the cultivation of an ethically and ritually disciplined life. Some Ru-ists extended the rigors of ceremonial court ritual

to social and family activities. Due to this phenomenon, Confucians have sometimes been thought of as traditionalists advocating traditional ritual court behaviors. It is interesting that Confucius in the *Analects* (7:1)[1] notes that he is a transmitter, not a creator.

2 The text, in truth, consists of fragments not written by Confucius himself but compiled by his disciples and second-generation disciples. The surviving text was probably made official at around the Western Han period. More recently, scholars have also turned their attention to another unearthed version believed to pre-date the well-accepted version.

3 The 499 short passages in the *Analects* are not systematically organized and repetitions and inconsistencies are common. Because it was written by a number of authors, there are several different interpretations of the key concepts in the *Analects*. It is possible to see differences between passages reflecting Confucius' ideas and others which have been modified or inserted at a later time. We may also treat the text as a source of insights into the intellectual history of Confucianism and of China more generally. Yet again, a good number of contemporary scholars—philosophers in particular—take the *Analects* as a text that is open-ended. These scholars continue to work on fresh commentaries and contemporary applications of ideas in the *Analects* text. Confucius emerges from the *Analects* as a committed, conscientious and skillful thinker. In many passages a range of people, including dukes and governors of villages, consult him on issues relating to good government and, more broadly, the good life, and passages show how Confucius takes various factors into consideration and how he balances them to arrive at a decision. Many first-time readers of the *Analects* are struck by the lack of basic normative principles or criteria upon which Confucius bases his decisions. For instance, in *Analects* 13:18[2], he expects sons and fathers to cover up for each other's misdeeds:

> The Governor of She in conversation with Confucius said, "In our village there is someone called 'True Person.' When his father took a sheep on the sly, he reported him to the authorities." Confucius replied, "Those who are true in my village conduct themselves differently. A father covers for his son, and a son covers for his father. And being true lies in this." (trans. Ames and Rosemont Jr 1998a: 166–167)[3]

---

1 子曰："述而不作，信而好古，窃比于我老彭。"

2 叶公语孔子曰："吾党有直躬者，其父攘羊，而子证之。" 孔子曰："吾党之直者异于是。父为子隐，子为父隐，直在其中矣。"

3 *The Analects of Confucius: A Philosophical Translation*, translated by Roger Ames and Henry Rosemont Jr (1998a), New York: Ballantine Books.

Some people feel at a loss to explain how Confucius, known widely as the founder of Confucian ethics, could make such immoral suggestion, and *Analects* (13:18) is often considered immoral because it approves lying. But if we continue to reflect on this passage, there are more questions we want to ask. These include: What were the punishments, if any, for theft? What was the worth of a sheep? How was the neighbor affected? What are the consequences for the child, if he reveals his father's theft, and if he doesn't? The situation of this child is a uniquely difficult one and presents no easy solution. It is futile to speculate on the "correct" answers to these questions. We should focus on more pertinent issues, such as the place of family and loyalty in ethical life, the ethical significance of relationships, the requirement to cover up for another, Confucius' method of moral consideration and its criteria.

4 Realistically, what Confucius is meant to have said to a duke about running a state, or how Confucius seats himself while eating, will have little relevance for us today. Perhaps we should not expect the *Analects* to provide normative answers to our ethical dilemmas. Instead, we might read it in order to understand the complexities associated with the process of moral reasoning as the early Confucians understood it. If this is correct, we may gain an understanding of how the Confucians studied the ancient texts (*Analects* 8:8; 1:15; 7:18; 8:3) [1]and learnt from experiences of enlightened people in the past (*Analects* 7:22)[2]. Seen in this light, the *Analects* is a collection of diary entries of other people's behaviors rather than a book of authoritative sayings or a comprehensive and systematic philosophical treatise. As the guidance of appropriate action and behavior, it can be used to generate and encourage reflective thinking about our own actions and commitments.

5 With this methodology in mind, let us examine one foundational concept in Confucianism, *ren* (humaneness). Together with *Li*, it crystallizes the Confucian ideal of cultivated humanism. Any understanding of Confucian philosophy rests on how we understand these two fundamental concepts and the interplay between them.

Ren (Humaneness)

6 *Ren* is mentioned only occasionally in texts pre-dating Confucius. In its earlier usage, the term referred to some manly or virile quality, particularly that of a king. For example, in two

---

1 子曰："兴于诗。立于礼。成于乐。"（8:8）子贡曰："贫而无谄，富而无骄，何如？" 子曰："可也。未若贫而乐，富而好礼者也。" 子贡曰："《诗》云，'如切如磋，如琢如磨。' 其斯之谓与？" 子曰："赐也，始可与言《诗》已矣！告诸往而知来者。"（1:15）子曰："不愤不启，不悱不发。举一隅不以三隅反，则不复也。"（7:18）曾子有疾，召门弟子曰："启予足！启予手！《诗》云：'战战兢兢，如临深渊，如履薄冰。' 而今而后，吾知免夫，小子！"（8:3）

2 子曰："三人行，必有我师焉。择其善者而从之，其不善者而改之。"（7:22）

hunting poems in the *Book of Poetry* (*Shi Jing*), *ren* refers to two huntsmen who are "handsome and *ren*" (Schwartz, 1985: 51)[1]. In the *Book of History* (*Shang Shu*), *ren* refers to the benevolent attitude of the ruler to his subjects. In the hands of the Confucians, however, the term gradually came to denote a moral quality characteristic of humanity. Hence, it is not surprising to find some variation in its use in early Confucian philosophy, to denote humanity in general, humaneness as a distinguishing characteristic of humanity, or the primary human virtue of compassion. This characteristic was referred to in many ways, but most commonly as an inborn disposition or a feature of collective socio-political life. The meaning of the concept is also revealed in its Chinese character: *ren* (仁) is comprised by two characters, the left signifying humanity (人) and the right, two (二). This suggests that the concept pertains to human relatedness. Hence, the term has been variously translated into English as benevolence, love, humaneness, humanity, human-heartedness, compassion and sympathy. Nevertheless, its meaning in the *Analects* is multifaceted and some more recent translations of *ren* avoid its identification with any one English term.

(Adapted and compiled from Karyn L. Lai, *An Introduction to Chinese Philosophy*)

Focus on the Content

I. Comprehension check.

Write T if the sentence is true, F if it is false, and NI if there is not enough information.

_________ 1. The *Analects*, written by Confucius, is the key text for Confucius ideas.

_________ 2. The *Analects* is unsystematic, repetitious and inconsistent.

_________ 3. Confucius sees himself primarily as a proponent of traditional ceremonial ritual.

_________ 4. By reading the *Analects*, people can have a general understanding of Chinese history.

_________ 5. According to the author, the *Analects* is a book of behavioral guidance rather than a philosophical one.

_________ 6. Since it is hard to find an accurate equivalent of "*ren*" in English, the best translation could be "*ren*" itself.

1 Schwartz, Benjamin (1985). *The World of Thought in Ancient China*. Cambridge: Belknap Press of Harvard University Press.

Ⅱ. Comprehension questions.

Answer the questions in complete sentences.

1. What reform did Confucius propose in time of confusion?
2. What is the main feature of Ru-ist education?
3. Based on the *Analects*, what kind of person is Confucius?
4. Why does Confucius say the true person is the one who covers for the other?
5. According to the author, how to read the *Analects*?
6. What does "*ren*" mean?

Ⅲ. Paraphrasing.

Paraphrase the underlined parts in the following sentences.

1. His proposal involved the elimination of the power abuse and exploitative behaviors of those in power.
2. Some people feel at a loss to explain how Confucius ..., could make such immoral prescriptions.
3. Seen in this light, the *Analects* is a collection of diary entries of other people's behaviors ...
4. Perhaps we should not expect the *Analects* to provide normative answers to our ethical dilemmas.
5. Together with *Li*, it crystallizes the Confucian ideal of cultivated humanism.
6. This suggests that the concept pertains to human relatedness.

Increase Language Proficiency

Ⅰ. Completion.

Complete the sentences below with the correct form from the box. The words can be used ONCE ONLY.

propose	involvement	conscience	consist of	ethical
realization	ceremony	sympathy	loyalty	eliminate
apply	abuse	identify		

1. Please don't stand on ________ (= Please be natural and relaxed) with me.
2. This diet claims to ________ toxins from the body.

3. They swore their ________ to the king.
4. Early ________ of a disease can prevent death and illness.
5. Is it ________ to promote cigarettes through advertising?
6. The situation was more complicated than they had at first ________.
7. Scientific discoveries are often ________ to industrial processes.
8. He has never really ________ with the aims of Animal Rights activists.
9. His ________ that the system should be changed was rejected.
10. What if he got a guilty ________ and brought it back?

Ⅱ. Sentence structure.

Study the grammatical structure of the following sentences.

1. Any understanding of Confucian philosophy rests on how we understand these two fundamental concepts and the interplay between them.
2. Realistically, what Confucius is meant to have said to a duke about running a state, or how Confucius seats himself while eating, will have little relevance for us today.
3. Hence, it is not surprising to find some variation in its use in early Confucian philosophy, to denote humanity in general, humaneness as a distinguishing characteristic of humanity, or the primary human virtue of compassion.

Ⅲ. Translation.

Translate the following sentences into Chinese/English.

1. His proposal involved the elimination of the power abuse and exploitative behaviors of those in power.
2. Ru-ist education consisted in the cultivation of an ethically and ritually disciplined life.
3. The process was to be initiated and led by leaders of society who were role models of broad education and ethical insight.
4. We may also treat the text as a source of insights into the intellectual history of Confucianism and of China more generally.
5. 子曰："学而时习之，不亦说乎？有朋自远方来，不亦乐乎？人不知而不愠，不亦君子乎？"（节选自《论语·学而》）（1:1）

Reflect on the Text

Ⅰ. Presentation.

Present one of the following topics to your class in a logical and clear way.

1. Based on your knowledge, please state what the Confucius' wisdom is in the *Analects*.
2. Please illustrate the different aspects of *ren/li* based on the remarks in the *Analects*.
3. What are the features of Chinese philosophy?

Ⅱ. Debate.

The class is to be divided into two groups and debate on the two different views on one of the following topics. State your point of view clearly and support your argument with convincing and substantial evidence.

1. Is there any practical significance in learning the *Analects* nowadays?
2. Is Confucius a philosopher?
3. Can "*ren*" be regarded as the Confucian Golden Rule?

Ⅲ. Comment.

Please comment on one of the following statements from the *Analects*.

1. Confucius remarked, "You should treat an enemy with decency and fairness; you should repay kindness with kindness."（子曰："何以报德？以直报怨，以德报德。"）（14:36）
2. Confucius remarked, "With plausible speech and fine manner will seldom be found moral character."（子曰："巧言令色，鲜矣仁"。）（1:3）
3. Confucius remarked, "Study without thinking is labour lost. Thinking without study is perilous."（子曰："学而不思则罔，思而不学则殆。"）（2:15）

Text B

The Apology of Socrates

1 For the sake of a little time, men of Athens, you will get a name and be charged with the responsibility, by those wishing to revile the city, for having killed Socrates, a wise man. For those wishing to reproach you will assert that I am wise, even if I am not. At any rate, if you had waited a short time, this would have come about for you of its own accord. For you see that my age is already far advanced in life and close to death. I say this not to all of you, but to those who voted to condemn me to death. I also say the following to these same ones.

2 Perhaps you suppose, men of Athens, that I have been convicted because I was at a loss for the sort of speeches that would have persuaded you, if I had supposed that I should do and say anything at all to escape the penalty. Far from it. Rather, I have been convicted because I was at a loss, not however for speeches, but for daring and shamelessness and willingness to say the sorts of things to you that you would have been most pleased to hear: me wailing and lamenting, and

doing and saying many other things unworthy of me, as I affirm—such things as you have been accustomed to hearing from others. But neither did I then suppose that I should do anything unsuitable to a free man because of the danger, nor do I now regret that I made my defense speech like this: I *Much* prefer to die having made my defense speech in this way than to live in that way. For neither in a court case nor in war should I or anyone else devise a way to escape death by doing anything at all. In battles it often becomes clear that one might escape death, at least, by letting go of his arms and turning around to supplicate his pursuers. And there are many other devices to escape death in each of the dangers, if one dares to do and say anything at all. But I suspect it is not hard, men, to escape death, but it is much harder to escape villainy. For it runs faster than death. And now I, since I am slow and old, am caught by the slower, while my accusers, since they are clever and sharp, are caught by the faster, by evil. And now I go away, condemned by you to pay the penalty of death, while they have been convicted by the truth of wretchedness and injustice. And I abide by my penalty, and so do they. Perhaps these things even had to be so, and I suppose there is due measure in them.

[3] Let us reflect and we shall see that there is great reason to hope that death is a good. Now being dead is either of two things—either it is a state of nothingness and utter unconsciousness, or, as men say, there is a change and migration of the soul from this world to another. If you suppose that there is no consciousness, but a sleep like the sleep of him who is undisturbed even by dreams, and were to compare the other nights and days of his own life with that night, and then were to tell how many days and nights in his own life he has lived better and more pleasantly than that night, then I suppose that the Great King himself, not to mention some private man, would not find such days and nights, when compared with the others. So if death is something like this, I at least say it is a gain; for eternity is then only a single night. On the other hand, if death is like a journey from here to another place, and if the things that are said are true, that in fact all the dead are there, then what greater good could there be than this, judges? For if one who arrives in Hades[1], released from those here who claim to be judges, will find those who are judges in truth—the very ones who are said to give judgment there, Minos[2]

1 In Greek mythology, Hades was a place under the earth where people went after they died.

2 A king of Crete for whom Daedalus built the Labyrinth to contain the Minotaur.

and Rhadamanthys[1], and Aeacus[2], and Triptolemus[3], and those of the other demigods who turned out to be just in their own lives—would this journey be a paltry one? Or again, to associate with Orpheus[4] and Musaeus[5] and Hesiod[6] and Homer[7], how much would any of you give? For I am willing to die many times if these things are true, since especially for myself spending time there would be wondrous: whenever I happened to meet Palamedes[8] and Telemonian Ajax[9], or anyone else of the ancients who died because of an unjust judgment, I would compare my own suffering with theirs. Above all, I shall then be able to continue my search into true and false knowledge; as in this world, so also in the next; and I shall find out who is wise, and who pretends to be wise, and who is not. What would not a man give, judges, to be able to examine the leader of the great Trojan expedition, or Odysseus[10], or Sisyphus[11], or numberless others, both men and women! To converse and to associate with them and to examine them there would be inconceivable happiness. Certainly those there surely do not kill on this account. For those there are happier than those here not only in other things but also in that they are immortal henceforth for the rest of time, at least if the things that are said are in fact true. But you too, judges, should be of good hope toward death, and you should think this one thing to be true: that there is nothing bad for

---

1 One of the judges of the dead in the underworld in Greek mythology.

2 A king of Aegina who, after he dies, becomes one of the three judges of the dead in the lower world, with Minos and Rhadamanthus.

3 A demi-god in Greek mythology. Demeter, the goddess of agricultural fertility and protector of marriage and women, sent him to teach mankind agriculture.

4 An ancient Greek legendary hero, a poet and lyre-player credited with the authorship of the poems forming the basis of Orphism. He married Eurydice and sought her in Hades after her death. He failed to win her back and was killed by a band of bacchantes.

5 An ancient Greek legendary poet.

6 A Greek poet in the 8th century BCE, whose existing works describe rural life and the family history of the gods and the beginning of the world.

7 An ancient Greek epic poet who is believed to have written the *Iliad* and the *Odyssey* (circa 850 BCE).

8 A prominent figure in the Trojan War, who was framed and accused of treasonable correspondence with the enemy, and then was stoned to death by Odysseus and Diomedes. He had a reputation for sagacity, and the ancients attributed a number of inventions to him, including the alphabet, numbers, weights and measures, coinage, board games, and the practice of eating at regular intervals.

9 A son of Telamon, king of Salamis, a grandson of Aeacus, who joined the expedition of the Greeks against Troy and killed himself in vexation when Achilles' armour was given to Odysseus.

10 One of the foremost of the Greek heroes at the siege of Troy, noted for his courage and ingenuity. His return to his kingdom of Ithaca was fraught with adventures.

11 A king of Corinth, punished in Hades for his misdeeds by eternally having to roll a heavy stone up a hill: every time he approached the top, the stone escaped his grasp and rolled to the bottom.

a good man, whether living or dead, and that the gods are not without care for his troubles. Nor have my present troubles arisen of their own accord, but it is clear to me that it is now better, after all, for me to be dead and to have been released from troubles. This is also why the sign did not turn me away anywhere, and I at least am not at all angry at those who voted to condemn me and at my accusers[1]. And yet it was not with this thought in mind that they voted to condemn me and accused me: rather, they supposed they would harm me. For this they are worthy of blame.

4 This much, however, I beg of them: when my sons grow up, punish them, men, and pain them in the very same way I pained you, if they seem to you to care for money or anything else before virtue. And if they are reputed to be something when they are nothing, reproach them just as I did you: tell them that they do not care for the things they should, and that they suppose they are something when they are worth nothing. And if you do these things, we will have been treated justly by you, both I myself and my sons. But now it is time to go away, I to die and you to live. Which of us goes to a better thing is unclear to everyone.

(Adapted and compiled from Thomas G. West, *Plato's Apology of Socrates: An Interpretation, with a New Translation.* Copyright by Cornell University, published by Cornell University Press.)

(From https://www.sjsu.edu/people/james.lindahl/courses/Phil70A/s3/apology.pdf)

Focus on the Content

I. Comprehension check.

Write T if the sentence is true, F if it is false, and NI if there is not enough information.

________ 1. It is not for his own sake, but for the sake of judges, that he is pleading.

________ 2. What Socrates says is to all the Athens.

________ 3. Socrates tells of what happens after death and he is troubled by death.

________ 4. Socrates was found guilty because he had made people believe what was true.

________ 5. Socrates believes to die is the highest virtue and can make one immortal.

________ 6. Socrates is indifferent to worldly success or possessions.

1 The prosecutors were Anytus, a democratic politician; and Meletus, a tragic poet; and Lykon, an obscure rhetorician. They maintained that Socrates was guilty of not worshipping the gods and further corrupting the young.

II. Comprehension questions.

Answer the questions in complete sentences.

1. Do you think Socrates was making an apology?
2. Why did Socrates make the speech?
3. How did Socrates view death?
4. Why did Socrates say death is a good thing?
5. What is the truth that Socrates believes in?
6. What kind of man is Socrates based on the excerpt?

III. Paraphrasing.

Paraphrase the underlined parts in the following sentences.

1. At any rate, if you had waited a short time, this would have come about for you of its own accord.
2. ... as I affirm—such things as you have been accustomed to hearing from others ...
3. But I suspect it is not hard, men, to escape death, but it is much harder to escape villainy. For it runs faster than death.
4. Certainly those there surely do not kill on this account.
5. This is also why the sign did not turn me away anywhere, and I at least am not at all angry at those who voted to condemn me and at my accusers.
6. Perhaps these things even had to be so, and I suppose there is due measure in them.

Increase Language Proficiency

I. Words in context.

Complete each sentence with the correct answer.

1. If a city is **reviled**, it is ________.
   A. criticized in an abusive or an insulting manner
   B. highly praised
2. If you **reproach** someone, you express your ________ with him or her.
   A. approval or appreciation
   B. disapproval or disappointment

3. If someone **is convicted of** a crime, he is found _________.

   A. guilty

   B. innocent

4. If one has no **consciousness** of anything, it shows he loses the ability to _________.

   A. perceive the surrounding things

   B. observe the surrounding things

5. If something is **paltry**, it is _________.

   A. significant

   B. insignificant

6. If you say someone is **immortal**, it shows his life_________.

   A. lasts forever

   B. will end

Ⅱ. Sentence structure.

Study the grammatical structure of the following sentences.

1. For the sake of a little time, men of Athens, you will get a name and be charged with the responsibility, by those wishing to revile the city, for having killed Socrates, a wise man.
2. To converse and to associate with them and to examine them there would be inconceivable happiness.
3. If you suppose that there is no consciousness, but a sleep like the sleep of him who is undisturbed even by dreams, and were to compare the other nights and days of his own life with that night, and then were to tell how many days and nights in his own life he has lived better and more pleasantly than that night, then I suppose that the Great King himself, not to mention some private man, would not find such days and nights, when compared with the others.

Ⅲ. Translation.

Translate the following sentences into Chinese.

1. For the sake of a little time, men of Athens, you will get a name and be charged with the responsibility, by those wishing to revile the city, for having killed Socrates, a wise man.
2. Perhaps you suppose, men of Athens, that I have been convicted because I was at a loss for the sort of speeches that would have persuaded you, if I had supposed that I should do and say anything at all to escape the penalty.

3. For neither in a court case nor in war should I or anyone else devise a way to escape death by doing anything at all.
4. Nor have my present troubles arisen of their own accord, but it is clear to me that it is now better, after all, for me to be dead and to have been released from troubles.
5. And yet it was not with this thought in mind that they voted to condemn me and accused me: rather, they supposed they would harm me. For this they are worthy of blame.

Reflect on the Text

Ⅰ. Presentation.

1. What type of person is Socrates? Does he resemble a Christian martyr?
2. How does Socrates think of wisdom? Is he a wise man? Please find out the relevant evidence in the text to support your view.
3. As one of the great ancient Greek philosophers, what does Socrates contribute to the world civilization?

Ⅱ. Debate.

Read the last part again: "... when my sons grow up, punish them, men, and pain them in the very same way I pained you, if they seem to you to care for money or anything else before virtue." Divide the class into two groups and debate on the two different views on one of the following topics. State your point of view clearly and support your argument with convincing and substantial evidence.

1. Happiness lies in the career success and accumulation of wealth.
2. Money is more important than virtue.
3. Money makes the mare go.

Ⅲ. Comment.

Comment on one of the following statements by Socrates from the *Apology*.

1. There's only one virtue—knowledge, and only one evil—ignorance.
2. Philosophy begins with an admission of ignorance.
3. Wealth does not bring about human excellence or virtue, but virtue makes wealth and everything else good for human beings.

Compare and Contrast

Ⅰ. Comparison.

Compare and contrast Socrates and Confucius, think about the similarities and the differences of the two great figures.

Ⅱ. Creative writing: "When Socrates meets Confucius"

In the Hades, Socrates met Confucius. They had a discussion on wisdom, knowledge, virtue, education and etc. Develop your imagination, design a setting and a plot for this unexpected encounter.

Ⅲ. Comment.

Socrates says, "The unexamined life is not worth living"; and Master Zeng (a disciple of Confucius) remarks, "I daily examine into my personal conduct on three points." Both stress on the importance of examination. however, they seem to emphasize different aspects. Please give your thoughts.

Unit 6

Food

Background

Food is central to all societies and with the development of society and the progress of human civilization diet is formed. Dietary culture is the sum of human dietary behavior, conception and its products formed in the process of human practice. The differences in dietary culture reflect differences in the larger cultures. They show different living environments, histories, value orientations in different nations. The traditional Chinese diet, featuring variety and abundance, is one among many traditional diet styles that has received praise for its flavor. Western diet which is considered unhealthy is characterized for an overconsumption of sugar, salt, and fat and protein from red meat. The present unit, regarding the developing trend of Chinese eating habits and the problems of American diet, helps people get to know what is a healthy diet and the importance of a healthy diet, ultimately encourages people to establish the awareness of healthy diet.

Text A

Chinese Diet Trends: Changing for the Better

1 The Chinese wellness consumer is attracting more and more attention. In line with growing incomes and education, the Chinese are starting to increase their focus on health and wellness. This can be seen particularly in terms of diet. With diet and nutrition playing such a major role in overall wellness, we decided to investigate the key trends in Chinese eating habits. We found a nation with major diet-related problems, but one that is now more health conscious and generally adjusting its diet in a positive direction.

2 Wellness and diet are closely tied to major trends in demographic and economic changes. Many of China's health and wellness trends can be directly traced back to the country's rising incomes and more affluent middle class. Credit Suisse reported China's middle class as including 109 million people in 2015, which is larger than that of the United States. McKinsey, meanwhile, predicts that the Chinese middle class will increase in size to 400 million people by 2020, with half of them being in the upper-middle-class segment, earning the equivalent of US $16,500–35,000 per year. China's transformation into a predominantly middle-class society is an extremely powerful social force with a corresponding impact on diet and wellness.

3 As China's economy opened up in the 1980s and consequently prospered, incomes rose

and more people moved to urban areas and joined the middle class. In line with this, people have shifted from their traditionally healthy, majorly plant-based diet and started eating much more meat, dairy products, salt, fat and sugar. This change in diet has had a significant negative effect on health.

4 However, what is happening right now—as incomes continue to rise and the population has become better educated—is that many people are now beginning to focus more on improving their health. This demographic trend of increased health consciousness is certain to continue to grow and develop in the coming years.

Obesity and diabetes (糖尿病) at critical levels

5 China is currently faced with a range of significant health problems stemming from a poor diet.

6 The country has the highest number of obese people in the world, with around 12% of adults classified as obese. 30% are overweight. Even amongst children, almost 10% are overweight and 6% are obese. This suggests a ticking time bomb of future health problems in China if major actions aren't taken to rectify the situation.

7 Back in the 1980s, when most of the country ate a basic and traditional Chinese diet, diabetes affected just 1% of the population. Following rapid income growth and a shift to a more unhealthy diet, the diabetes rate has since shot up to 11% of the population. China now hosts the most diabetics in the world. There were 109 million diabetics in China in 2015, a third of all those suffering from the disease. This number is predicted to increase to 150 million by 2040. In addition to this, almost 500 million Chinese people are currently estimated to be pre-diabetic.

8 The financial costs are huge. Around 13% of all of China's medical costs are considered as related to diabetes, and it has been estimated that by 2030 this will reach US $47 billion.

Taste for fast food changing fast

9 China has witnessed a boom in fast food consumption. In 2011, Yum! Brands, the parent company of KFC, announced that half of its global profit of US $1.8 billion came from China. KFC now has more than 6,000 stores across the country, bringing in US $5 billion in revenue in 2017. McDonald's has been opening 10 stores per week.

10 However, more recent trends are showing a significant decline in growth of fast food consumption. As the middle class has become more sophisticated in their eating habits, fast food has lost its appeal. In an attempt to meet this change in preference, fast food restaurants are

offering healthier options. For example, KFC now allows consumers to choose for their food to be grilled rather than deep-fried.

11 Despite this, fast food sales are predicted to grow only 2% in 2019, the slowest segment in the overall food service industry.

Rapid growth in meat consumption slowing down

12 Since the 1980s, China's consumption of meat has boomed from around 1 million tons to over 8 million tons in 2010. In the early 1980s, the average Chinese person ate around 13.6 kg of meat per year. This has now ballooned to 63.5 kg per person per year—however, this remains just half the amount of an average US citizen.

13 A recent report from Rabobank, though, states that Chinese meat consumption growth is expected to markedly slow down due to changes in consumer behavior.

Sugar in a sweet spot, but more than a pinch less salt needed

14 Sugar is one of the most important food ingredients in terms of health. It is directly blamed for health issues such as obesity and diabetes, diseases that, as mentioned above, are major health issues in modern China. Despite this, China's consumption of sugar is significantly below the global average. Sugar has not been a major part of traditional Chinese diets, although it has certainly increased over the past couple of decades. According to the FAO, there are regional differences in Chinese sugar consumption, with the South of China having the highest consumption levels. In addition, unsurprisingly, rural areas have lower consumption levels than urban areas. Despite this, recent trends show increases in sugar consumption in rural areas and a declining trend of sugar consumption in urban areas.

15 Sugar consumption growth in China has been weak in the past few years and was expected to remain relatively stable for 2018–2019; however, a global sugar production surplus has pushed prices low, which may stimulate greater consumption. Despite this, the long-term trend is one of moderation primarily due to health concerns and the use of sweetener replacements.

16 While sugar consumption in China is far below the global average, the opposite is true in terms of salt. A study published in *The Lancet* reports that salt consumption in China is amongst the highest in the world. The researchers reported that 80% of communities had a mean sodium consumption of greater than five grams per day, significantly higher than the 3–5 grams per day in most other countries. Chinese salt consumption is twice the level recommended by the World Health Organization and double the amount an average US resident consumes. This may be an important cause of the fact that around a third of Chinese adults suffer from hypertension, which leads to heart

attacks and strokes, the top two causes of death in China. Because of this, salt is high on the Chinese health agenda in terms of its negative health effects and the need for reduced consumption.

17 Salt consumption is, however, on a downward trend. This is mainly due to changes in diet and greater use of refrigeration for food preservation. A study by UNICEF and China's official food safety institution found that salt consumption in China dropped 22% between 2000 and 2009–2011. In spite of this, sodium intake only declined 12% during the same time due to significant consumption of pickled vegetables and seasonings such as soy sauce, as well as increased consumption of processed foods.

Soft drinks decline while alcohol increases

18 Patrick Healy, Managing Director of Swire Beverages, recently told the *South China Morning Post* that Chinese consumers are increasingly opting for healthier drink options. He says that they are shunning classic soft drinks and are, instead, focusing on premium packaged waters and energy drinks. While traditional soft drinks will continue to grow at single-digit rates, he says that newly emerging drinks products will grow at double-digital percentages. Steven Kwok, Associate Partner at OC&C Strategy Consultants, adds to this, forecasting that low sugar, sugar-free and low calorie drinks "will become dominant."

19 However, in terms of alcohol, the trend is for an increase. While sales of *baijiu*, China's most popular alcohol, fell by 20% from 2017, beer sales have grown 31%. Whisky and wine sales are also reportedly growing. China's high levels of alcohol consumption have led to the country coming out top in terms of alcohol-related deaths according to *The Lancet*. This is mostly attributable to men, with three times more men drinking alcohol than women. In fact, the alcohol-related health effects for women are far lower than the world average.

Major health challenges but heading in the right direction

20 With the Chinese middle class being such a powerful global force, their diet and consumptions trends are important to study. Our investigation shows that over the past couple of decades, Chinese diets have worsened, with increased consumption of meat, fast food, sugar and processed foods. This has led to major health crises in terms of obesity, diabetes, strokes and heart attacks. More recent diet trends, however, show positive changes to fast food, salt, sugar and soft drinks consumption. Chinese people are increasingly concerned about eating both safe and healthy foods, and companies in the wellness sector should aim to cater to these desires.

(Adapted from *Chinese Diet Trends: Changing for the Better* accessed to at https://gocohospitality.com/chinese-diet-trends/)

Focus on the Content

I. Comprehension check.

Write T if the sentence is true, F if it is false, and NI if there is not enough information.

_______ 1. Chinese people's health consciousness is becoming stronger with growing incomes and education.

_______ 2. By 2020 China's middle class will be larger than that of the United States according to the text.

_______ 3. The increase of Chinese middle class has had a positive impact on Chinese diet and wellness.

_______ 4. China's high diabetes rate stems from an unhealthy diet.

_______ 5. KFC witnessed its peak profit of US $5 billion in China in 2017.

_______ 6. KFC's catering to Chinese customers taste promoted fast food sales.

_______ 7. China's consumption of meat now is still lower than that of the United States.

_______ 8. Obesity and diabetes are directly connected to too much sugar intake.

_______ 9. High salt consumption in China is an important reason for heart attacks and strokes.

_______ 10. Compared with *baijiu*, sales of beer, whisky and wine are growing currently in China.

II. Multiple choice.

Choose the best answer to each question.

Detail 1. The following factors change the Chinese diet in a bad way EXCEPT _______.

A. the rise of incomes

B. increasing number of the middle class

C. growing education

D. more consumption of salt, fat and sugar

Detail 2. Which statement is right for sugar consumption in China?

A. Chinese sugar consumption is one of the highest in the world.

B. Sugar is an important ingredient of traditional Chinese diets.

C. Urban areas have lower consumption levels than rural areas.

D. The consumption levels are different in different regions.

Inference 3. What can be inferred from the statement in Para. 16–Para. 17 about salt consumption and sodium intake?

A. There is a close connection between salt consumption and sodium intake.

B. There is no necessary connection between salt consumption and sodium intake.

C. Sodium is a part of salt.

D. Sodium intake has a limited impact on health.

Detail 4. What's the problem for traditional soft drinks?

A. They contain too much sugar.

B. They contain carbon dioxide.

C. They contain low calorie.

D. They are less tasteful.

Gist 5. What is the purpose of the author in writing the passage?

A. To introduce the Chinese diet to the readers.

B. To introduce the problems with the Chinese diet.

C. To provide guidance on eating in China.

D. To draw related institutions' attention to the Chinese recent diet trends.

Detail 6. Which of the following statements is true according to the passage?

A. Recent positive changes to a poor diet attribute to the improvement of health consciousness.

B. The alcohol-related health effects for Chinese are far lower than the world average.

C. Chinese major diet-related problems have been solved.

D. The growth in meat consumption will cause many diseases.

Ⅲ. Comprehension questions.

Answer the questions in complete sentences.

1. What happened to the Chinese diet habits with incomes rising, more people moving to urban areas and the middle class increasing?
2. Compared with the early 1980s, how much has China's consumption of meat per person per year increased?
3. Why did sodium intake decline slowly compared with salt consumption at the same period?

4. Why does the growth of fast-food consumption in China decline recently?
5. Why is it estimated that sugar consumption will remain moderate in the long run?
6. What are the reasons for the downward trend of salt consumption?

Increase Language Proficiency

I. Words in context.

Complete each sentence with the correct answer.

1. If you say that someone or something is on the cusp, you mean they are about to be in a particular ________.
   A. state B. condition C. way D. order
2. When you ________ food, you cook it using very strong heat directly above or below it.
   A. fry B. grill C. steam D. stew
3. When something ________, it increases rapidly in amount.
   A. explodes B. balloons C. bursts D. blooms
4. Sweetener is a kind of ________ substance that can be used in drinks instead of sugar.
   A. artificial B. natural C. active D. harmful
5. Premium goods are of a higher than usual ________ and are often expensive.
   A. nutrition B. value C. productivity D. quality
6. If you shun someone or something, you deliberately ________ them.
   A. mislead B. criticize C. avoid D. destroy

II. Completion.

Complete the sentences below with the correct form of words from the box.

estimate	agenda	preservation	obesity	affluent
moderation	opt	adjust	conscious	epidemic

1. Drinking alcohol in ________ is beneficial to the heart, a new study has revealed.
2. In America, a lot of what we eat has led to ________ and has led to a real change in sort of what our diet is in the last 30 years.

3. Unless you _________ for a prepaid plan, there's no way of telling how much a phone will really cost you.
4. They think that economic development and _________ of the environment can go hand in hand.
5. _________ disease is often in connection with bad sanitary conditions.
6. Childhood education and literacy targets are rightly a high priority on the global health and social _________.
7. They _________ China's private aircraft market could grow by up to 25 percent a year over the next 10 years.
8. Only the _________ countries have been able to organize such entities, both in the public and the private sector.
9. You will quickly _________ yourself to student life.
10. A patient who is not fully _________ should never be left alone.

Ⅲ. Translation.

Translate the following passage into English.

从过去到现在，判断饮食或饮食计划好坏的标准都是根据食物的营养成分及其生化成分。然而，随着现代农业和食品加工的发展，我们食品的营养在下降，我们的健康变得更糟。化肥和杀虫剂使劣质作物进入市场，食品加工夺走了我们食物的营养和活力，而过于忙碌的生活方式也为快餐进入人们的生活提供了契机。

____

____

____

____

____

Reflect on the Text

Ⅰ. Presentation.

Chinese dietary culture is extensive and profound with its diversification. Different regions in China have their own diet habits. Would you like to introduce the eating habits in your hometown? Please make a presentation in class.

Ⅱ. Debate.

Nowadays in order to pursue a healthy diet, some people choose to be vegetarians. But it is said that vegetarians lack nutrition and are easily threatened by diseases with reduced body resistance. Do you think we should take vegetarian eating habits? Please make a debate on it.

Ⅲ. Comment.

China has long tradition of drinking tea. However, coffee has become a popular choice of Chinese young people and now more and more Chinese people begin to drink coffee. Please make some comments on it.

Text B

What's Wrong with the American Diet?

By Chris Woolston

1 What's wrong with the typical American diet? This is what the experts have to say: "Too many calories," says Marion Nestle, PhD, MPH, Professor of Nutrition and Food Studies at

New York University. "Too many calories," asserts Melanie Polk, registered dietitian and former director of nutrition education for the American Institute of Cancer Research. Barbara Gollman, a registered dietitian who used to be the spokesperson for the American Dietetic Association, weighs in with her own theory: "Too many calories."

2 Perhaps it's time to stop talking about fatty foods and admit that we simply eat too many calories. Twenty-five years ago, the average American consumed about 1,850 calories each day. Since then, our daily diet has grown by 304 calories (roughly the equivalent of two cans of soda). That's theoretically enough to add an extra 31 pounds to each person every year. Judging from the ongoing obesity epidemic, many Americans are gaining those pounds—and then some.

3 Take the latest national surveys on weight. More than 68 percent of all Americans are considered overweight or obese, according to the Centers for Disease Control and Prevention. (This means they have a body mass index greater than 25.)

4 But calories don't tell the whole story. To truly understand what's wrong with the American diet, you have to know how we manage to consume all those calories. There are two possible ways to go overboard: You can eat too many calorie-dense foods, or you can eat too much food or beverages in general. Many people choose to do both. Our fondness for fast food is taking a particularly heavy toll. Although the federal government recommends that we have at least two to five cups of fruits and vegetables a day, for example, surveys show that the average American eats only three servings a day, and 42 percent eat fewer than two servings a day.

5 Here's a closer look at our love affair with calories—and the health crisis it has created.

The carnival mirror

6 Of course, there is no single American diet. We all have our individual tastes, quirks, and habits. Still, experts see clear patterns in our food choices. In fact, most American diets fall into one of two broad categories: "Western" or "prudent."

7 The prudent diet is a nutritionist's dream. People in this category tend to eat relatively large amounts of fish, poultry, cruciferous vegetables (i.e. cabbage and broccoli), greens, tomatoes, legumes, fresh fruits, and whole grains. They also skimp on fatty or calorie-rich foods such as red meats, eggs, high-fat dairy products, French fries, pizza, mayonnaise, candy, and desserts.

8 The Western diet is the prudent diet reflected in a carnival mirror. Everything is backwards: red meat and other fatty foods take the forefront, while fruits, vegetables, and whole grains are pushed aside. In addition to fat and calories, the Western diet is loaded with cholesterol, salt, and sugar. If that weren't bad enough, it's critically short on dietary fiber and many nutrients—as well

as plant-based substances (phytochemicals) that help protect the heart and ward off cancer.

9 Put it all together and you have a recipe for disaster. In a 12-year study of more than 69,000 women, published in the *Archives of Internal Medicine*, a Western diet was found to significantly raise the risk of coronary heart disease. Other studies have shown that a high-fat, low-nutrient diet increases the likelihood of colon cancer, diabetes, and a host of other ailments.

Portion distortion

10 The Western diet is nothing new. The typical American family in the 1950s was more likely than we are to sit down to a meal of pork chops and mashed potatoes than stir-fried tofu and broccoli. So why has the obesity epidemic exploded in the last 20 years? It's a matter of size. "Twenty years ago, the diet wasn't as varied as it is today, and people didn't eat nearly enough fruits and vegetables," Gollman says. "But the portions were more in line with what people really need."

11 From bagel shops to family restaurants to vending machines to movie theater concession stands to the dining room table, our meals and snacks are taking on massive proportions. "Everyone in the food industry decided they had to make portions larger to stay competitive, and people got used to large sizes very quickly," Nestle says. "Today, normal sizes seem skimpy."

12 The excess of our diet is especially obvious away from home. "Look through the window of any of the big chain restaurants, and you'll see huge platters of food coming out of the kitchen," Polk says. One of those platters could easily pack 2,000 calories, enough to last most people all day.

Convenience culture

13 Despite our national obsession with weight loss, the obesity epidemic continues to be a national health concern. The human craving for fats and sweets will never go away, and it's getting easier than ever to satisfy those cravings. With 170,000 fast-food restaurants and 3 million soft-drink vending machines spread across the country, huge doses of calories are never far away—especially when those soda machines are sitting right in the middle of public schools.

14 In 1978, for example, the typical teenage boy in the United States drank about seven ounces of soda a day, according to *Fast Food Nation* author Eric Schlosser. Today, he drinks nearly three times that much, getting a whopping 9 percent of his daily calories from soda. Teenage girls are close behind.

15 Perhaps not surprisingly, studies show that childhood obesity has hit epidemic proportions over the last few decades. The main culprits, according to experts: high-fat foods, sodas, and too little exercise.

Taking control

16 Fatty, unbalanced, and oversized: That, in a nutshell, is the American diet. But it doesn't have to be your diet. "People think eating healthy is a difficult task, but small things make a big difference," Polk says. "You just have to employ some important strategies. It's called taking charge."

17 If you eat more than four meals away from home each week, you can start by making healthy choices as you dine. "As we eat at restaurants more and more, we have to take control of these outlandish meals," Polk says. Order foods that have been baked, steamed, or grilled instead of deep-fried. Have your salad dressing or other fatty toppings served on the side, and if mayonnaise isn't low-fat, skip it entirely. Consider ordering a salad and an appetizer instead of an entree. If you do order an entree, plan to take at least half of it home with you.

18 No matter where you eat, try to stick to a few basic guidelines. The amount you should eat depends on your age and activity level—teenage boys and men need to eat more than young children, for example. Aim for three to eight ounces of bread, cereal, rice, or pasta each day, the more whole grains the better. This isn't quite as daunting as it sounds—one cup of rice counts as two ounces, and a single slice of bread counts as one ounce. Two to five cups of fruits and vegetables each day will give you fiber and vital nutrients; if you're using a plate, try to cover half of it in produce. (One serving is a medium piece of fruit, a half cup of chopped fruit, a half cup of chopped vegetables, or a cup of fresh greens.) Taken together, fruits, vegetables, and grains can satisfy your hunger and fuel your body without blowing your calorie budget.

19 Meat isn't forbidden, but try to think of it as a complement to your meals, not the main attraction. According to the U.S. Department of Agriculture (USDA) food pyramid, you only need two servings (up to six and a half ounces) from the "meat group" each day. The group includes meat, poultry, fish, dry beans, eggs, and nuts. It goes without saying that six ounces of salmon, pinto beans, or chicken breast is preferable to six ounces of marbled steak (a serving of meat, by the way, should be about the size of a deck of cards).

20 Much of the advice can be boiled down to one word: moderation. By eating different foods from every part of the pyramid and watching your portion size, you can make your own personal American diet healthy and nutritious. We have more choices and more temptations than ever before, but ultimately, we also have the final say over what we eat. Take control, and enjoy.

(Adapted from *What's Wrong with the American Diet?* by Chris Woolston accessed to at https://docslib.org/Whats-Wrong-With-The-American-Diet)

Focus on the Content

I. Comprehension check.

Write T if the sentence is true, F if it is false, and NI if there is not enough information.

1. The average American eats only 3 cups of fruits and vegetables a day.
2. American diet belongs to the category of "Western".
3. The Western diet with high fat and low nutrient is likely to cause many diseases.
4. The excess of American diet in restaurants is more serious than home.
5. Today teenage girls consume soda much more than 1978.
6. Tofu and milk belong to "meat group".
7. Not eating meat is the best way to manage your diet.

II. Multiple choice.

Choose the best answer to each question.

Detail 1. Americans intake such many calories in all the following ways EXCEPT _________.

A. they eat too many high-calorie foods

B. they eat too much food

C. they eat few fruits and vegetables

D. they drink too many beverages

Inference 2. What's the meaning of "The Western diet is the prudent diet reflected in a carnival mirror." in Para. 8?

A. Western diet is a prudent diet.

B. Western diet is the opposite of the prudent diet.

C. To some extent, Western diet is a prudent diet.

D. Western diet is a nutritionist's dream.

Detail 3. Which is the proper description for the prudent diet?

A. Red meat and fatty foods can't be found in the prudent diet.

B. The prudent diet is short on dietary fiber.

C. The prudent diet tends to be the fat- and cholesterol-controlled diet.

D. The prudent diet shares some similarities with the Western diet.

Detail 4. Why are Americans pursuing large portions?

A. In order to meet people's need.

B. It can make food industry competitive.

C. People get used to large sizes.

D. In order to offer enough nutrition for people.

Vocabulary 5. The following words can generalize the American diet EXCEPT ________.

A. fatty

B. unbalanced

C. oversized

D. nutrient

Detail 6. Which behavior falls into "taking charge"?

A. Do not order deep-fried foods.

B. Do not eat meat.

C. Do not order salad and entree.

D. The more fruits and vegetables the better.

Gist 7. What is the purpose of the author in writing this passage?

A. To criticize the American diet habits.

B. To point out the problems with the American diet.

C. To draw Americans' attention to their diet and call on them to eat healthy.

D. To give some suggestions to the American diet.

Ⅲ. Comprehension questions.

Answer the questions in complete sentences.

1. Now how many calories does the average American consume each day?
2. What are the differences between Western diet and prudent diet?
3. What is the reason for the explosion of obesity epidemic in the last 20 years?
4. What makes the obesity epidemic a national health concern?
5. What has caused childhood obesity epidemic in last few decades?
6. How many ounces do three slices of bread count as?
7. How to make personal American diet healthy and nutritious?

Increase Language Proficiency

Ⅰ. Words in context.

Complete each sentence with the correct answer.

1. If you say that something takes a heavy toll, you mean that it brings a lot of ________.

   A. convenience　B. suffering　C. pleasure　D. happiness

2. If you crave something, you want to ________ it very much.

   A. throw　B. sell　C. have　D. change

3. If you describe an amount as whopping, you are emphasizing that it is ________.

   A. small　B. large　C. medium　D. heavy

4. According to Para. 7, a prudent diet is ________ diet.

   A. popular　B. simple　C. nutritious　D. natural

5. Nutrients are ________ that help plants and animals to grow.

   A. fertilizers　B. substances　C. minerals　D. vitamins

6. A concession is a special ________ that is given to someone.

   A. favor　B. deal　C. privilege　D. treat

7. Something that is daunting makes you feel slightly ________ about dealing with it.

   A. eager　B. enthusiastic　C. anxious　D. worried

Ⅱ. Completion.

Complete the sentences below with the correct form of words from the box.

outlandish	budget	overboard	ward	skimp
culprit	dose	obsession	servings	ailments

1. Workers at the nuclear plant were exposed to a high ________ of radiation.
2. About 10% of Japanese teenagers are overweight. Nutritionists say the main ________ is increasing reliance on Western fast food.
3. An idea that seems ________ to one generation becomes commonplace to the next.
4. The parents were active campaigning against cuts to the education ________.
5. His ________ with music didn't prevent him from indulging in his other favorite activities: sports and cards.

6. Pick something relatively hard to do for you, but do not go ________.
7. This recipe will be enough for four ________.
8. Such a thin padded coat cannot ________ off the cold mountain wind.
9. The pharmacist can assist you with the treatment of common ________.
10. Many old people ________ on food and heating in order to meet their bills.

Ⅲ. Translation.

Translate the following passage into English.

一项研究表明，保持一周的高脂肪、高糖饮食就可能影响大脑中某个负责情绪、学习、记忆和动机的器官。即便一个身体健康、身材苗条的人，吃一周西餐也会影响大脑功能，使他们难以控制食欲。此外，研究证明，糖果、小吃和巧克力等可口食物在饱腹时变得更有吸引力。这样看来，西方饮食习惯使人们很难抗拒暴饮暴食。

____

____

____

____

____

____

Reflect on the Text

Ⅰ. Presentation.

Please give a brief introduction to the origins and evolution of the Western diet.

Ⅱ. Debate.

As overweight or obesity among American kids and teens becomes more and more serious, people think that laws should be made to reduce junk food consumption. Please make a debate on "Should Junk Food Be Illegal?".

Ⅲ. Comment.

As we all know, fast food is unhealthy. But with the influence of Western diet, more Chinese young people prefer fast food compared with traditional Chinese food. Please make some comments on "Western Fast Food in China".

Compare and Contrast

Ⅰ. Presentation.

Chinese and Western diet are rooted in different cultural backgrounds. Please make a presentation on "Cultural Differences between Chinese and Western diet".

Ⅱ. Comment.

With the spread of Western diet culture in China, it is found that the western diet mode, diet ideas, diet wares, diet habits and so on are immersing into Chinese traditional diet culture subconsciously. To some extent Chinese diet culture is showing Western characteristics. What attitude should we hold to the effect? Please make a comment on it.

Unit 7

Places of Interest

Background

Travel has been essential to our lives. It can broaden our horizons, expand our knowledge, refresh our minds, enrich our experiences, purify our souls, boost our spirits...Obviously, the benefits we can gain from travel are too many to be counted. And those benefits are more noticeable when we visit a royal palace, which is very often, far beyond a scenic spot, the very embodiment of national consciousness, character, memory, and identity. To a certain extent, it may serve as a sort of window into the nation where it is built. That is what we will encounter in the present unit regarding two royal palaces—the Forbidden City (known as the Palace Museum since 1925) and Buckingham Palace, both of which are among the five most renowned royal palaces in the world. By reading the two texts, we will be impressed by the architectural wonders the two palaces have represented and informed of the historical, political and cultural vicissitudes they have witnessed.

Text A

The Palace Museum

1 Established in 1925, the Palace Museum is located in the imperial palace of the consecutive Ming (1368–1644) and Qing (1644–1911) dynasties. The magnificent architectural complex, also known as the Forbidden City, and the vast holdings of paintings, calligraphy, ceramics, and antiquities of the imperial collections make it one of the most prestigious museums in China and the world. In 1961, the State Council designated the former imperial residence as one of China's foremost-protected cultural heritage sites, and in 1987 it was listed as a UNESCO World Heritage site.

Location and Layout

2 Situated in the heart of Beijing, the Palace Museum is approached through the Gate of Heavenly Peace. Immediately to the north of the Palace Museum is Prospect Hill, while on the east and west are the Wangfujing and Zhongnanhai neighborhoods. Ancient China's astronomers endowed the location with cosmic significance. They correlated the emperor's abode, which they considered the pivot of the terrestrial world, with the Pole Star—believed to be the center of the heavens. Because of its centrality and restricted access, the palace was called the Forbidden City. It was built from 1406 to 1420 by the third emperor of the Ming Dynasty, the Yongle Emperor

who, upon usurping the throne, determined to move his capital northward from Nanjing to Beijing. Over 200 years later, the Ming Dynasty fell to the Qing dynasty in 1644. Then, in 1911, the Qing were subsequently overthrown by republican revolutionaries. The last emperor Puyi continued to live in the palace after his abdication until he was expelled in 1924. During nearly five hundred years of imperial operation, the palace served as the residence and court of twenty-four emperors.

3 The Forbidden City is surrounded by 10-metre-high walls and a 52-metre-wide moat. Measuring 961 meters from north to south and 753 meters from east to west, the complex covers an area of 1,120,000 square meters. Each side of the rectangular city has a gate. These four gates are the Meridian Gate on the south, the Gate of Divine Prowess on the north, and the East and West Prosperity Gates, respectively. Entering from the south, visitors will see a succession of halls and palaces spreading out on either side of the central axis. The glowing yellow roofs of the stately buildings seem to levitate above the vermilion walls. This magnificent sight is amplified by the painted ridges and carved beams of the ancient structures.

4 Known as the Outer Court, the southern portion of the Forbidden City features three main halls—the Hall of Supreme Harmony, Hall of Central Harmony, and Hall of Preserving Harmony. These three halls are flanked by the Belvedere of Embodying Benevolence and Belvedere of Spreading Righteousness. The Outer Court was the venue for the emperor's court and grand audiences.

5 Mirroring this arrangement is the Inner Court, which is the northern portion of the Forbidden City. The Palace of Heavenly Purity, Hall of Union, and Palace of Earthly Tranquility lie upon the central axis. The Six Eastern Palaces and the Six Western Palaces are private imperial residences found on their respective sides of the main axis. Other major buildings in the Inner Court include the Hall for Abstinence and Hall of Sincere Solemnity in the east and the Hall of Mental Cultivation, Belvedere of Raining Flowers, and Palace of Compassion and Tranquility in the west. The Inner Court is not only comprised of the residences of the emperor and his consorts but also venues for religious rituals and administrative activities. The far north end of the Inner Court is the Imperial Garden.

6 In total, the buildings of the two courts account for an area of some 163,000 square meters. These structures were designed in strict accordance to the traditional code of architectural hierarchy, which designated specific features to reflect the paramount authority and status of the emperor. Ordinary mortals were forbidden—and most would never dare—to come within close proximity to this imperial city.

Founding

7 The Xinhai Revolution of 1911 ended with the abdication of the last emperor Puyi. The provisional government allowed him to continue to live in the Inner Court of the Forbidden City. Meanwhile, all of the imperial treasures from palaces in Jehol and Mukden were moved to the Forbidden City for public display in the Outer Court in 1914. In 1924, during a coup launched by the warlord Feng Yuxiang, Puyi was finally expelled from the Forbidden City. The management of the palace fell to a committee that was set up to deal with the concerns of the deposed imperial family. That committee also audited the imperial collections. After a year of tireless preparations, on 10 October 1925, the committee arranged a grand ceremony in front of the Palace of Heavenly Purity to mark the inception of the Palace Museum. According to a twenty-eight-volume inventory published in 1925, the treasure trove left by the Qing imperial family numbered more than 1,860,000 items. All these were divided into separate collections. Exhibition halls were opened to display some of the treasures.

Collection Evacuation

8 Shortly before the outbreak of World War Ⅱ, the Japanese had annexed territory in China's northeast and proceeded to march on Beijing. With this looming threat, the Museum's authorities decided to evacuate its collection rather than let it fall into enemy hands or risk destruction in battle. In the frantic time from February to May 1933, the most important pieces in the collection were packed into 13,427 crates and sixty-four bundles and sent to Shanghai in five batches. In 1936, they were dispatched to Nanjing where a depository had been built and a branch of the Palace Museum was to be established.

9 On 7 July 1937, shots fired at the Lugou Bridge heralded the eruption of the War of Resistance Against Japanese Aggression in all directions. Within a year, the Japanese had invaded most of eastern China. The treasures stored in Nanjing had to be moved again—this time by three routes to Sichuan, where they were secreted in Baxian, Emei, and Leshan. Only at the end of the war were they consolidated in Chongqing and subsequently returned to Nanjing in 1947. With the imminent victory of the Communist army south of the Yangtze River, the weakened Kuomintang began their retreat to Taiwan. From the end of 1948 to 1949, the Kuomintang selected 2,972 crates to be shipped across the Strait for storage in Taichung. The contents of these crates formed the collection of the Taipei Palace Museum, which opened to the public in 1965. Most of the national treasures remaining in Nanjing were gradually returned to Beijing, although to this day 2,221 crates remain in storage in Nanjing.

10 During this tumultuous decade of war and revolution, none of the treasures were lost or damaged, in spite of the incredible quantity of antiquities. This was largely due to the steadfast commitment of the Palace Museum staff, whose achievement in preserving these treasures was nothing short of heroic. Unfortunately, as a result of this long period of upheaval, some of the treasures were dispersed into various institutions. In the early 1950s, shortly after the establishment of the People's Republic of China, the Palace Museum staff was imbued with new determination and enthusiasm to restore the Forbidden City to its former glory. The Museum's administration launched a policy of comprehensive restoration. All the tall structures were equipped with lightning rods, while modern systems were installed to ensure fire protection and security. Additionally, the maintenance of the surrounding moat has been a distinct government priority, particularly since the beginning of the reforms instituted during the early 1980s.

Development

11 Although the Forbidden City used to be an impenetrable fortress, the imperial palace is now a public museum. With rich collections representing the broad spectrum of 5,000 years of Chinese civilization and the 600-year history of the Forbidden City, the Palace Museum has seen many developments since its founding in 1925 and looks forward to carrying on the legacy of the past for future generations. Now, as always, the Palace Museum is committed to the preservation of national heritage and the goal of serving as a model for museums around the world.

(Adapted from *About the Palace Museum* accessed to at https://en.dpm.org.cn/about/about-museum/2015-01-20/1615.html)

Focus on the Content

I. Comprehension check.

Write T if the sentence is true, F if it is false.

________ 1. In 1987, the Summer Palace was listed as a UNESCO World Heritage site.

________ 2. The Inner Court was the place for emperors to live with their families.

________ 3. After the Xinhai Revolution, Puyi was expelled from the Forbidden City.

________ 4. No treasures from the Palace Museum have been left in Nanjing.

________ 5. The Palace Museum staff's achievement in preserving these treasures was not heroic at all.

Ⅱ. Comprehension questions.

Answer the questions in complete sentences.

1. What was special about the location of the Forbidden City?

2. What were the functions of the Inner Court?

3. Why were the treasures in the Palace Museum moved to other places before 1945?

4. How many places had those treasures been moved to between 1933–1949?

5. After 1949, how was the Palace Museum restored?

Ⅲ. Matching.

Match the years with the statements. Write the correct letters in brackets.

( ) 1. 1914 A. The Palace Museum was founded.

( ) 2. 1924 B. The most important treasures in the Palace Museum were sent to Shanghai.

( ) 3. 1925 C. The treasures were sent to Nanjing.

( ) 4. 1933 D. Puyi was eventually driven out of the Forbidden City.

( ) 5. 1936 E. All of the imperial treasures from palaces in Jehol and Mukden were moved to the Forbidden City.

Increase Language Proficiency

Ⅰ. Words in context.

Choose A or B that explains the word in bold.

1. With the **imminent** victory of the Communist army south of the Yangtze River, the weakened Kuomintang began their retreat to Taiwan.

   A. inevitable B. approaching

2. The glowing yellow roofs of the stately buildings seem to **levitate** above the vermilion walls.

   A. float B. level

3. Shortly before the outbreak of World War Ⅱ, the Japanese had **annexed** territory in China's northeast.

   A. occupied B. found

4. Only at the end of the war were they **consolidated** in Chongqing.

   A. strengthened B. joined

5. This was largely due to the steadfast **commitment** of the Palace Museum staff.

   A. cooperation B. dedication

Ⅱ. Vocabulary expansion: Word forms.

Complete the table with the correct forms of the words and then choose the right word form for each sentence below.

VERB	NOUN	ADJECTIVE	ADVERB
evacuate		/	/
amplify			
		accessible	
/	hierarchy		
/			subsequently

1. The only __________ to the building is along that muddy track.
2. One hundred __________ spent the night at a school during the storm.
3. It's a very __________ organization in which everyone's status is clearly defined.
4. __________ to their arrival in Chicago, they bought a new car.

5. They had __________ money for the trip.

Ⅲ. Translation.

Translate the following passage into English.

紫禁城坐落于北京市中心，又称故宫，是明清时期的皇宫。这座矩形宫殿是世界上最大的宫殿群。四周环绕着六米深的护城河和十米高的城墙。四面各有一门。护城墙四角各有一个精心建造的独特角楼。紫禁城被分成两部分：南面的部分即外朝，是皇帝行使最高权力的地方；而北面的部分即内廷，是皇帝和皇室成员生活的地方。今天，紫禁城敞开大门，迎接国内外游客。

Reflect on the Text

Ⅰ. Presentation.

Act as a guide to introduce the Forbidden City to other students.

Ⅱ. Debate.

Do you think Puyi should be expelled from the Forbidden City? Why or why not?

Ⅲ. Comment.

Comment on the architectural philosophy that underlies the Forbidden City.

Text B

Buckingham Palace

1 Buckingham Palace has served as the official London residence of the UK's sovereigns since 1837 and today is the administrative headquarters of the monarch. Although in use for the many official events and receptions held by the King, the state rooms at Buckingham Palace are open to visitors every summer. Buckingham Palace has 775 rooms. These include 19 State Rooms, 52 royal and guest bedrooms, 188 staff bedrooms, 92 offices and 78 bathrooms. In measurements, the

building is 108 meters long across the front, 120 meters deep (including the central quadrangle) and 24 meters high.

History of Buckingham Palace

2 George Ⅲ bought Buckingham House in 1761 for his wife Queen Charlotte to use as a comfortable family home close to St James's Palace, where many court functions were held. Buckingham House became known as the Queen's House, and 14 of George Ⅲ's 15 children were born there. George Ⅳ, on his accession in 1820, decided to reconstruct the house into a pied-à-terre, using it for the same purpose as his father George Ⅲ. As work progressed, and as late as the end of 1826, the King had a change of heart. With the assistance of his architect, John Nash, he set about transforming the house into a palace. Parliament agreed to a budget of £150,000, but the King pressed for £450,000 as a more realistic figure. Nash retained the main block but doubled its size by adding a new suite of rooms on the garden side facing west. Faced with mellow bath stone, the external style reflected the French neo-classical influence favored by George Ⅳ.

3 The remodeled rooms are the State and Semi-State Rooms, which remain virtually unchanged since Nash's time. The north and south wings of Buckingham House were demolished and rebuilt on a larger scale with a triumphal arch—the Marble Arch—as the centerpiece of an enlarged courtyard, to commemorate the British victories at Trafalgar and Waterloo. By 1829 the costs had escalated to nearly half a million pounds. Nash's extravagance cost him his job, and on

the death of George Ⅳ in 1830, his younger brother William Ⅳ took on Edward Blore to finish the work. The King never moved into the Palace. Indeed, when the Houses of Parliament were destroyed by fire in 1834, the King offered the Palace as a new home for Parliament, but the offer was declined.

4 Queen Victoria was the first sovereign to take up residence in July 1837 and in June 1838 she was the first British sovereign to leave from Buckingham Palace for a Coronation. Her marriage to Prince Albert in 1840 soon showed up the Palace's shortcomings. A serious problem for the newly married couple was the absence of any nurseries and too few bedrooms for visitors. The only solution was to move the Marble Arch—it now stands at the north-east corner of Hyde Park—and build a fourth wing, thereby creating a quadrangle. The cost of the new wing was largely covered by the sale of George Ⅳ's Royal Pavilion at Brighton. Blore added an attic floor to the main block of the Palace and decorated it externally with marble friezes originally intended for Nash's Marble Arch. The work was completed in 1847. By the turn of the century the soft French stone used in Blore's East Front was showing signs of deterioration, largely due to London's notorious soot, and required replacing. In 1913 the decision was taken to reface the façade. Sir Aston Webb, with a number of large public buildings to his credit, was commissioned to create a new design. Webb chose Portland Stone, which took 12 months to prepare before building work could begin. When work did start it took 13 weeks to complete the refacing, a process that included removing the old stonework.

5 The present forecourt of the Palace, where Changing the Guard takes place, was formed in 1911, as part of the Victoria Memorial scheme. The gates and railings were also completed in 1911; the North-Centre Gate is now the everyday entrance to the Palace, whilst the Central Gate is used for State occasions and the departure of the guard after Changing the Guard. The work was completed just before the outbreak of the First World War in 1914.

Buckingham Palace Today

6 Today, Buckingham Palace is very much a working building and the centerpiece of the UK's constitutional monarchy, serving as the venue for many royal events and ceremonies from entertaining foreign Heads of States to celebrating achievements at investitures and receptions.

7 More than 50,000 people visit the Palace each year as guests to State banquets, lunches, dinners, receptions and Garden Parties. The King also holds weekly audiences with the Prime Minister and receives newly-appointed foreign Ambassadors at Buckingham Palace.

8 Receptions are held at the Palace throughout the year to recognize the work of industry,

government, charities, sport, the Commonwealth and many more areas of life. For example, in 2015, The Queen hosted a reception for players, organizers and supporters of the Rugby World Cup.

9 Buckingham Palace is often a focal point for significant national celebrations and commemorations. In 2002, a music concert was staged in the garden of Buckingham Palace to mark the Queen's Golden Jubilee, which included an unforgettable performance of "God Save the Queen" by Brian May from the roof of the Palace and at Her Majesty's Diamond Jubilee celebrations in 2012 members of the public were invited to have a special picnic in the Buckingham Palace Garden.

10 The balcony of Buckingham Palace is one of the most famous in the world. The first recorded Royal balcony appearance took place in 1851, when Queen Victoria stepped onto it during celebrations for the opening of the Great Exhibition. Since then, Royal Balcony appearances have marked many occasions from the Queen's annual official birthday celebrations to watch the RAF Flypast at the end of Trooping the Color, Royal Weddings, as well as special events of national significance such as the 75th anniversary of the Battle of Britain.

11 Whilst Buckingham Palace is seen as the administrative hub of the monarchy, it is also very much a family home and many Royal Weddings have been celebrated at Buckingham Palace, most recently the Duke and Duchess of Cambridge's.

12 The offices of those who support the day-to-day activities and duties of the King and their immediate family, such as the Private Secretary's Office and the Privy Purse and Treasurer's Office are located at Buckingham Palace.

(https://www.royal.uk/royal-residences-buckingham-palace)

Focus on the Content

I. Comprehension check.

Write T if the sentence is true, F if it is false.

________ 1. In 1761 George Ⅲ bought Buckingham Palace for his wife Queen Charlotte.

________ 2. After the wedding, Queen Victoria and Prince Albert lived in Buckingham Palace comfortably.

________ 3. London's air pollution might have caused harm to the buildings there.

________ 4. Sir Aston Webb owned a number of large public buildings.

________ 5. Buckingham Palace had been the seat of Parliament.

Ⅱ. Blank filling.

Fill in the blanks with proper information according to the text.

1. Today Buckingham Palace is the ________ of the monarch.
2. Queen Victoria's ________ took place in 1838.
3. ________ was used to celebrate British victories in the Napoleonic Wars.
4. At Buckingham Palace the Queen also receives ________ ambassadors.
5. The forecourt of the Palace is where ________ takes place.

Ⅲ. Matching.

Match the years with the statements. Write the correct letters in brackets.

( )	1. 1830	A. The 50th anniversary of the Queen's accession was celebrated.
( )	2. 1837	B. The first recorded Royal balcony appearance took place.
( )	3. 1851	C. The present forecourt of the Palace was formed.
( )	4. 1911	D. Blore was employed by William Ⅳ to continue the transformation.
( )	5. 2002	E. Queen Victoria moved into the Palace.

Increase Language Proficiency

Ⅰ. Words in context.

Choose A or B that explains the word in bold.

1. The remodeled rooms remain **virtually** unchanged since Nash's time.
   A. usually B. actually
2. The north and south wings of Buckingham House were **demolished.**
   A. knocked down B. put up
3. By 1829 the costs had **escalated** to nearly half a million pounds.
   A. increased B. decreased
4. Sir Aston Webb was **commissioned** to create a new design.
   A. ordered B. encouraged
5. Buckingham Palace is seen as the administrative **hub** of the monarchy.
   A. place B. center

Ⅱ. Vocabulary expansion: Word forms.

Complete the table with the correct forms of the words and then choose the right word form for each sentence below.

VERB	NOUN	ADJECTIVE	ADVERB
/	extravagance		
/		sovereign	/
transform			/
	deterioration	/	/
attach			/

1. The building underwent various ________ over the years.
2. Please see the document ________.
3. The ________ of a country refers to its independent and autonomous power and control.
4. We knew that, for the children's sake, we had to prevent our relationship from ________ any further.
5. The film is notable for its ________ settings and special effects.

Ⅲ. Translation.

Translate the following words or phrases into Chinese.

1. neo-classical

____

____

2. constitutional monarchy

____

____

3. pied-à-terre

____

____

4. façade

____

____

Reflect on the Text

Ⅰ. Presentation.

Act as a tour guide to introduce Buckingham Palace to other students.

Ⅱ. Debate.

According to Text A, Puyi was expelled from the Forbidden City. Do you think British Kings or Queens should also be expelled from Buckingham Palace? Why or why not?

Ⅲ. Comment.

In what sense is Buckingham Palace seen as the administrative hub of the monarchy and a family home?

Compare and Contrast

Ⅰ. Presentation.

List the differences and similarities between the Palace Museum and Buckingham Palace.

Ⅱ. Comment.

Comment on the influence of political systems on a nation's palace architecture by referring to the information offered in the present unit.

Unit 8

Health

Background

In this unit, we will read two passages about health. Health means the conditions of one person's body or mind, so there are two kinds of health with equal importance: physical health and mental health.

The first passage focuses on physical health. In current society, people have known well the key role of adopting a healthy lifestyle. A healthy body is the base of mental health, regular work, and a cheerful mood. Not only the elderly, but also more and more younger people have realized the significance of body health. Many companies have noticed this and developed some new kinds of tonics to attract younger consumers. We will know more details on physical health and diet therapy in the first passage.

The second passage focuses on mental health. Mental health is an essential part of overall health and well-being. Mental health includes our emotional, psychological, and social well-being. It affects how we think, feel, and act. It also helps determine how we handle stress, relate to others, and make healthy choices. Mental health is vital at every stage of life, from childhood and adolescence through adulthood. We will learn some ways to better cope with anxiety and maintain our mental health in the second passage.

Text A

Too Busy to Be Tired, Too Tired to Be Busy

By Zhang Lei

1 In the 1970s the Western world gorged itself on fad diets, from Atkins to Scars-dale, and the millions of books about them that were sold helped keep the publishing industry in good shape. About the same time, punk rock music made its world debut.

2 Turn the clock forward half a century, and dieting and punk have been sewn seamlessly together—in China of all places—to give us pengke yangsheng, the punk diet.

3 Of course, the thing about fad diets is that often what they most have going for them is a catchy name, and that may well apply to the punk diet. In fact strictly speaking the name seems to describe a lifestyle—an attitude even—rather than a food regime, even if it does relate to what one consumes. Also, as with many new fangled phenomena like this in China, its genesis, or at least the name, seems to have been conceived in cyberspace.

4 But let's take ourselves away from the internet for a moment and into the real world, and talk about how one can spot a punk dieter. Consider these three pictures: In one hand a young

man holds a thermos flask cup with steam pouring out of it, and in the other he holds a glass half full of scotch on the rocks. After staying up for half the night and catching a lot fewer than forty winks a young woman sits there applying the most expensive face pack to her visage. A group of three hits the disco floor, ostensibly to keep fit, and between dances imbibes whiskey soaked in goji berries.

5 So unlike a conventional diet that runs a straight line emphasizing healthy eating and engaging in physical activity, the punk diet, championed by Generation Z, those born this century, bounces back and forth between extremes, its practitioners taking great delight not only in the irony but in the fact that they are leading an oh-so trendy lifestyle as well.

6 However, when you delve below the thin surface of all this, you find that young people do seem to have piled on themselves—or had piled on them—such a weighty load of academic and work pressures that it is no wonder that at such an early age they have cottoned on to the idea that they had better start caring for their health, too.

7 Last year *National Health Insight Report* said that of the four age groups, the post 1960s, 70s, 80s and 90s, the younger the person was, the dimmer the view they had of their personal health.

8 "On the one hand is fast-paced work and life generally, and on the other is anxiety about losing one's competitive edge," says Jiang Wenxiu of the Department of Psychiatry, Zhongda Hospital, Southeast University in Jiangsu province.

9 "Young people always seem to feel that they must do something to defend their hairline, or to resist the fine lines that climb up around the corners of their eyes."

10 A survey last year by the market consultancy iResearch found that among young people who stay up late at night nearly 42.6 percent usually go to sleep between 10 pm and 11 pm, and nearly 33.7 percent between 11 pm and 12 am. The rest, 23.7 percent, said they go to sleep after midnight and have long-term problems relating to irregular work and rest.

11 Seventy percent of the late sleepers said they could sleep seven hours a day, and nearly 8 percent said they suffered from severe sleep deprivation, with average sleep of five hours or less. In addition, a comparison of groups with different times for going to sleep found that the earlier the time, the higher the proportion of full sleep (seven hours or more), and the later the time of going to sleep, the greater the proportion of severe sleep deprivation (five hours or less).

12 "It has almost become routine among young office workers to binge drink coffee when they are busy at work," Jiang says. "They ponder the dark circles under their eyes, and an instant later you see them putting goji berries into the thermos flask they bought in Japan."

13 Jiang light-heartedly sums up the health regimen of contemporary young people: "They spend half their life skinny dipping and the other half magic potion sipping."

14 And healthcare companies, always with an eye to marketing opportunities, have spotted this phenomenon. Among them is Tong Ren Tang medicine store, 351 years young, in Beijing. It has created what it calls a "Chinese medicine coffee" that taps into demand and the very name of the new sounds like a health preservation.

15 That Tong Ren Tang should have decided to become involved in this young mark fits in well with the irony of the punk diet lifestyle, for when many people think of this company what would no doubt cross their minds would be pictures of the quaint old stores in which it plies its wares, the surroundings including carved wooden beams and paintings, old-fashioned containers full of medicine and almost invariably an ancient Chinese doctor with silver hair and white beard.

16 Tong Ren Tang, one of the most prestigious traditional medicine stores in China, was founded in 1669, the eighth year of the Kangxi Reign in the Qing Dynasty (1644–1911), and from 1723 was dedicated to imperial medicine, serving the needs of eight emperors over 188 years.

17 Goji berry latte, appetizing Americano, mother-wort rose latte, diuretic anti-swelling osmanthus honey bean coffee are some of the oh-so-non-traditional drinks it sells.

18 "We soften the goji berry, squeeze it into a pulp and add it to the coffee," says Li Shengli, barista of Tong Ren Tang Coffee Shop. "What it does is nourish the liver and kidney. For those who often stay up late it's a good idea to drink wolfberry latte."

19 Li, a barista for many years, says that after to work for Tong Ren Tang this year, he realized that he could understand coffee from the perspective of Chinese medicine. The coffee itself that relieves pain is matched with Chinese herbs such as wolfberry, tangerine peel and cinnamon, high in potassium and antioxidants.

20 However, herbal coffee is just the tip of the iceberg of the company's stronger attention to young consumers. At Tong Ren Tang Zhima Health No 1 Store in Chaoyang district of Beijing, the first floor of the store also offers packaged retail products such as health soup, congee and pastry bread; on the second floor is the traditional drug store, where registration, consultation and medicine are available.

21 Su Xiaohang, in charge of brand promotion, says the herbal coffee is not the focus of the marketing, but it hopes to use coffee and fast-moving consumer goods to attract people to create a new environment that reflects healthy living.

22 "In the normal course of events a person feels sick, goes and sees a doctor, has their pulse taken, is given some medicine and goes home," Su was quoted as saying in a recent interview with China News Service.

23 "We plan to emphasize the equal importance of medicine and food and help people through diet therapy."

24 A recent iResearch report on health consumption trends among young people found that more than 90 percent of those born this century have a general awareness of the importance of health, more than half of them taking practical steps to do something about it for themselves.

25 The first step on this road to looking after one's health, of course, is to equip oneself with whatever is healthy. Someone who follows a punk diet and who is doing a lot of overtime might drench themselves in a cup of vigor-enhancing ointment to replenish vitality, chew two pieces of donkey-hide gelatin cake to take care of a bad complexion, drink a cup of instant white fungus soup to moisten bone-dry skin, or eat a few black sesame pills if strands of their hair seem to fall out at the mere touch of a finger.

26 Recently CBNData, Alibaba Health and Tmall Appliances jointly published a report titled *New Foodism*, according to which sales of traditional tonics grew more than 20 percent in 2018 and 2019, and which says that those born in the 1990s have become the main buyers of online of traditional tonics over the past three years.

27 "We have always considered health products as a market for the elderly, but as people's economic well-being continues to improve, the care that the young have for managing their image and looking after their physical health is conducive to the rise of young people's health products," says Guo Xin, a marketing professor at Beijing Technology and Business University.

28 According to the market research company Euromonitor International, China's healthcare products industry turned over 162.7 billion yuan last year, 9.8 percent more than in 2018. The domestic health care products market is reckoned to be worth 100 billion yuan, it says, and analysts say that more and more companies are getting into the market because of the rising awareness of young people of the importance of good health.

(From *Too busy to be tired, too tired to be busy* by Zhang Lei accessed to at https://www.chinadaily.com.cn/a/202010/31/WS5f9cd12da31024ad0ba82494_1.html)

Focus on the Content

Ⅰ. Comprehension check.

Write T if the sentence is true, F if it is false.

________ 1. The punk diet is a newly born concept but has gained much popularity among young generations.

________ 2. It was reported that younger people cared more about their health and had a clearer view towards their personal health than older people.

________ 3. Some young people have no choice but to stay up late because of their irregular work.

________ 4. Some traditional brands with a long history have shown great interest in the punk diet but they don't agree that this is a healthy lifestyle.

________ 5. The elderly have become the main buyers of online of traditional tonics over the past three years.

Ⅱ. Multiple choice.

Choose the best answer to each question.

Gist 1. Which of the following words has less relation with the punk diet?

A. a lifestyle

B. an attitude

C. physical activity

D. consumption

Detail 2. According to the passage, which is the time period when most young people who stay up late usually go to bed?

A. between 10 p.m. and 11 p.m.

B. between 11 p.m. and 12 a.m.

C. between 1 a.m. and 2 a.m.

D. having irregular rest

Inference 3. Which statement is NOT true about the diet therapy?

A. It could attract more people to buy such kind of food and stimulate the economy.

B. It shows the market's attention to young consumers.

C. It emphasizes that food could replace medicine sometimes.

D. It could urge more people to care about their health at an earlier age.

Inference 4. In the fifth paragraph, it is mentioned that the punk diet is unlike a conventional diet that runs a straight line emphasizing healthy eating and engaging in physical activity. Based on this, which of the following is more persuasive?

A. This doesn't mean that the punk diet is unhealthy but means that the punk diet emphasizes healthy eating only.

B. This doesn't mean that the punk diet is unhealthy but means that the punk diet is non-traditional.

C. This means that the punk diet is unhealthy and pays less attention to physical activity.

D. This means that the punk diet is unhealthy but emphasizes physical activity.

Gist 5. Which one of the following reasons has not been mentioned to explain the rising awareness of good health among young people?

A. The fast-paced work and life make young people nervous and tired.

B. Anxiety from work such as worrying about losing one's competitive edge.

C. The care that the young have for managing their image.

D. Various advertisements and attractive packages.

Ⅲ. Comprehension questions.

Read the text carefully and answer the following questions.

1. In the fourth paragraph, three pictures are imagined. What is the purpose of such a description?
2. "The post 1960s, 70s, 80s and 90s, the younger the person was, the <u>dimmer</u> the view they had of their personal health." (7th paragraph) What does the underlined word mean here?
3. According to the passage, how could people understand coffee from the perspective of Chinese medicine?
4. Could you find and list some food a person who follows a punk diet would buy according to the passage? And what features do those food have?
5. What could be the most possible effect of the diet therapy based on the passage?

Increase Language Proficiency

I. Explanation.

Explain the underlined word or expression in each sentence in your own words.

1. The thing about fad diets is that often what they most have going for them is a catchy name, and that may well apply to the punk diet.
2. When you delve below the thin surface of all this, you find that young people do seem to have piled on themselves…
3. On the one hand is fast-paced work and life generally, and on the other is anxiety about losing one's competitive edge.
4. They ponder the dark circles under their eyes, and an instant later you see them putting goji berries into the thermos flask they bought in Japan.
5. However, herbal coffee is just the tip of the iceberg of the company's stronger attention to young consumers.

II. Sentence completion.

Complete the sentences below with the correct form of words in brackets.

1. I could spend each day _________ (gorge) on chocolate.
2. Their new _________ (fangle) doll hit stores just a few years later in 1902.
3. The _________ (ostensibly) reason for his absence was illness.
4. He _________ (imbibe) elements of oriental mysticism from the years he spent in India.
5. It is _________ (irony) that she became a teacher—she used to hate school.
6. I suddenly _________ (cotton) on to what he was doing.
7. I did remember, but only _________ (dim).
8. In the inner cities you would find neglected children suffering from social _________ (deprive).
9. They conducted a _________ (vigor) campaign against tax fraud.
10. He _________ (moist) his lips before he spoke.

III. Translation.

Translate the following paragraph into Chinese.

The first step on this road to looking after one's health, of course, is to equip oneself with whatever is healthy. Someone who follows a punk diet and who is doing a lot of overtime might drench themselves in a cup of vigor-enhancing ointment to replenish vitality, chew two pieces of donkey-hide gelatin cake to take care of a bad complexion, drink a cup of instant white fungus soup to moisten bone-dry skin, or eat a few black sesame pills if strands of their hair seem to fall out at the mere touch of a finger.

Reflect on the Text

Ⅰ. Explanation.

The passage mentions that contemporary young people "spend half their life skinny dipping and the other half magic potion sipping". Please explain the meaning of the underlined part.

Ⅱ. Expression.

According to the passage, do you think what the author's attitude towards the punk diet and health products is? Please give your reasons.

Ⅲ. Point of View.

Have you, your friends or families ever bought any dietary supplement? Do you think such kind of food really has some effects? Please express your thoughts with some real examples.

Text B

Lost Touch:
How a Year Without Hugs Affects Our Mental Health

By Eleanor Morgan

1 There's only so much a dog can do, even if that is a lot. I live alone with my staff, and by week eight of the first lockdown she was rolling her eyes at my ever-tightening clutch. I had been sofa-bound with COVID-19 and its after-effects before lockdown was announced, then spring and summer passed without any meaningful touch from another person. I missed the smell of my friends' clothes and my nephew's hair, but, more than anything, I missed the groundedness only another human body can bring. The ache in my solar plexus that married these thoughts often caught me off guard.

2 The need for touch exists below the horizon of consciousness. Before birth, when the amniotic fluid in the womb swirls around us and the foetal nervous system can distinguish our own body from our mother's, our entire concept of self is rooted in touch. "The human body has built all its models based on touch received from caregivers," says Dr Katerina Fotopoulou, a professor of psychodynamic neuroscience at University College London. "We're utterly reliant on the caregiver to satisfy the body's core needs. Little can be done without touch."

3 Nina Smith is 40, and lives alone in south London. She experienced a protracted recovery after a spinal injury in 2018, requiring long periods of bed rest. People visited, but her pain levels meant that being touched was difficult. She felt she had good foresight for how to prepare for the first lockdown. "I thought I knew how it would play out," she says over Zoom. "For example, I knew how strict I had to be about the routine of going for walks; you always feel slightly better having taken in different surroundings." But after six weeks, her resolve started to crumble. "The isolation I'd already experienced made me more vulnerable than I'd realised. I tried to keep myself in a routine but..." she begins to cry. "At some point, not being able to have a hug was genuinely torturous. I don't believe the government considered the impact of the first lockdown on people living alone."

4 As adults, we may not comprehend the importance of touch even when it disappears. "We might begin to realise that something is missing, but we won't always know that it's touch," says Prof Francis McGlone, a neuroscientist based at Liverpool John Moores University and a leader in the field of affective touch. "But when we talk about the problem of loneliness, we often ignore the obvious: what lonely people aren't getting is touch."

5 Touch has a huge impact on our psychological and physical wellbeing, says Prof Robin Dunbar, an evolutionary psychologist at the University of Oxford. "With our close friends and family, we touch each other more than we realise," he says. As adults, Dunbar's research has found, we have a core set of, on average, five friends who we can call on as a shoulder to cry on. "We see exactly the same thing in primates," he says. "Even in much bigger primate societies, groups of five best friends appear at every layer, who do all their grooming together—their form of social touch. In primates and humans, these intense coalitions act as a buffer; they keep the world off your back." It is unsurprising, then, that of the 40,000 people from 112 countries who took part in a 2020 BBC and Wellcome Collection survey, the three most common words used to describe touch were: "comforting", "warm" and "love".

6 As the pandemic continues, many of us will be trying to cope with profound stress without the comfort of touch. We all have different needs and boundaries (McGlone says "not everyone suffers from a lack of touch; I don't really like being cuddled, and drive my poor wife nuts"), but the total absence of touch, particularly when emotions are high, contravenes the hardwiring that regulates us from our preverbal years.

7 "Touch is a modulator that can temper the effects of stress and pain, physical and emotional. We have seen in our research that a lack of touch is associated with greater anxiety," says Fotopoulou. "In times of high stress—the loss of a job, or a bereavement, for example—

having more touch from others helps us cope better, particularly in calming the effects of [the stress hormone] cortisol." Even if we're used to not being touched a lot, after a while the need can feel very physical—sometimes described as "skin hunger" or "touch hunger".

8 While I can empathise with the exhausting monotony my friends with young families have described to me (and I know that the grass is always greener), I have felt the lack of belonging to a pack acutely. Claire Birke, a teacher from Edinburgh, has felt it, too: "I'm 37, and most of my friends are living with partners or children," she says. "I have never felt more aware of my single status, nor the lack of intimate bodily contact, in my life."

9 The number of people in the UK living on their own went up by 16% to 7.7 million between 1997 and 2017. The sliver of sociability that came with social bubbles being announced has felt life-saving. Smith has been "bubbling" with a couple who live together and says it has helped with her mood. But the days are long, and her friends "are not particularly tactile".

10 "I realise how much I touch people without thinking," she says. "I feel like I am holding all this emotion in my body with nowhere to put it."

11 In high-stress states, it can feel as if our bodies can barely contain our emotion if there's no one there to hold us. "Lots of studies support the theory that touch gives the brain a signal that it can delegate its resources for coping because someone else is there to bear the brunt. This relaxes the body, going some way to restoring the stress budget, if you like," says Fotopoulou. But touch is not a single sense. The two square metres of skin that contain us are teeming with nerve fibres that recognise temperature, texture and itch, etc. One set of fibres exists purely to register gentle, stroking touch: the C tactile afferents (CTs). McGlone has been studying this since 1995, when it was discovered in humans. "These neurons, in the skin of all social mammals, transmit slow electrical signals to the emotional processing parts of the brain. They play a critical role in developing the social brain and our ability to withstand stress."

12 The highest density of CTs across the body are in the parts we can't "groom" ourselves, such as the shoulders and back. "If you love having your back rubbed it's because there are more CTs there," says McGlone. "Stimulation of these neurons releases oxytocin and dopamine, and has a direct impact on cortisol levels, which regulates our mood." In 2017, Fotopoulou's team published a study that showed even gentle, slow stroking from a stranger can reduce feelings of social exclusion. But in our normal lives, we're not going round stroking each other all the time. "No, you don't need that touch all day," McGlone says. "We only need this gentle kind of touch intermittently."

13 In these times of touch deprivation there is no real substitute for what we get from other

humans, but there are ways to soothe ourselves. Fotopoulou's lab will soon publish a study conducted during the pandemic that builds on the theory that, in the same way we think we can feel others' pain, we may be able to experience touch vicariously, too. Researchers have found that seeing touch (on TV or in films, for example)—particularly social, affective or pet touch—can give us some of the benefits of feeling touch. "This is called 'vicarious touch'," says Fotopoulou. "The brain codes multisensory experiences in multiple ways. We can also 'feel' the pain and pleasures of others just by 'seeing' them," she says. "This is not a permanent or complete substitute, but a partial one."

14 Products such as weighted blankets can help. Smith says that laying one across her chest and shoulders makes her feel "much calmer"—speaking, perhaps, to an instinctive need to stimulate the CTs. Interacting with animals is also settling. "My neighbour's cat has decided to live with me half the time and having her sat on my chest, purring, is so soothing."

15 This resonated: the warmth of my dog's back under my hand has been the most grounding thing for me over the last 12 months. I know this feels good, but why? "When you're stroking your dog, you're engaging systems that would be activated if the dog was stroking you," says McGlone.

16 A hunger for touch is a signal that a primitive need is not being met. But evolution is on our side. Every scientist I spoke to was hopeful that, once we can come together again, we will adjust quickly. "It will differ between people, probably based on the duration people have been alone, and there may be a period of clumsiness and renegotiation," says Dunbar. "But we have evolved to adapt."

(From *Lost touch: how a year without hugs affects our mental health*
by Eleanor Morgan in *The Guardian* 2021/1/24)

Focus on the Content

I. Comprehension check.

Write T if the sentence is true, F if it is false.

_________ 1. Before birth, the foetal nervous system cannot distinguish our own body from our mother's.

_________ 2. As adults, we could better comprehend the importance of touch when it disappears.

________ 3. If one person is surrounded by friends, he would also feel lonely if he could not be touched by other people, such as a hug, for a long time.

________ 4. Animals in much bigger primate societies would have similar social patterns like humans.

________ 5. Some research has proved that a lack of touch is associated with greater anxiety.

Ⅱ. Multiple choice.

Choose the best answer to each question.

Detail 1. According to the passage, some research has found that on average a person has a core set of ________ friends.

A. four B. five

C. six D. twelve

Detail 2. In the 13th paragraph, there is one sentence: This is not a permanent or complete substitute, but a partial one. What does "a partial one" mean here?

A. a gentle kind of touch B. a weighted blanket

C. seeing touch D. pet touch

Gist 3. Which of the following could not be provided by touch?

A. Calming the effects of stress

B. Having a sense of belonging to a pack acutely

C. Feeling that our bodies can contain our emotion

D. feeling others' pain

Inference 4. Which of the following statements is NOT true according to the passage?

A. In a 2020 BBC and Wellcome Collection survey, the three most common words used to describe touch were: "comforting", "warm" and "peaceful".

B. Hug has a huge impact on our wellbeing, both psychologically and physically.

C. Touch could help people better cope with things with greater stress.

D. It could be inferred that hug or touch has a vital influence for mammals specially.

Reference 5. Which is NOT the basic elements for mammals to cope with stress through touch?

A. social life B. neurons C. green grass D. brain

Ⅲ. Comprehension questions.

Read the text carefully and answer the following questions.

1. Why can the foetal nervous system distinguish our own body from our mother's?
2. What is one of the reasons that could explain people's relaxation after having their backs rubbed?
3. Why does the author mention the dog in the 1st and 15th paragraphs twice?
4. Why could people feel comfortable when they only see touch?
5. In the 5th paragraph, there is one sentence: these intense coalitions act as a buffer; they keep the world off your back. What is the meaning of the underlined part?

Increase Language Proficiency

Ⅰ. Explanation.

Explain the underlined word in each sentence in your own words.

1. I live alone with my staff, and by week eight of the first lockdown she was rolling her eyes at my ever-tightening clutch.
2. In 2017, Fotopoulou's team published a study that showed even gentle, slow stroking from a stranger can reduce feelings of social exclusion.
3. Before birth, when the amniotic fluid in the womb swirls around us and the foetal nervous system can distinguish our own body from our mother's, our entire concept of self is rooted in touch.
4. She felt she had good foresight for how to prepare for the first lockdown.
5. As the pandemic continues, many of us will be trying to cope with profound stress without the comfort of touch.

Ⅱ. Sentence completion.

Complete the sentences below with the correct form of words in brackets.

1. She stood there, the flowers still ________ (clutch) in her hand.
2. I can't remember any more—I must have lost ________ (conscious).
3. Businesses have become increasingly ________ (rely) on complicated computing systems.
4. The eldest son is being ________ (groom) to take over after his father retires.

5. This material ________ (crumble) very easily.

6. She looked very ________ (vulnerability) standing there on her own.

7. They were imprisoned and ________ (deprivation) of their basic rights.

8. The hot summer days were ________ (temper) by a light breeze.

9. I am ________ (acute) aware of the difficulties we face.

10. The ceremony was ________ (transmission) live by satellite to over fifty countries.

Ⅲ. Translation.

Translate the following paragraph into Chinese.

"Touch is a modulator that can temper the effects of stress and pain, physical and emotional. We have seen in our research that a lack of touch is associated with greater anxiety," says Fotopoulou. "In times of high stress—the loss of a job, or a bereavement, for example—having more touch from others helps us cope better, particularly in calming the effects of [the stress hormone] cortisol." Even if we're used to not being touched a lot, after a while the need can feel very physical—sometimes described as "skin hunger" or "touch hunger".

Reflect on the Text

Ⅰ. Explanation.

The passage tells us that "products such as weighted blankets can help". Could you explain this with what we have learned from the passage?

Ⅱ. Expression.

According to the passage, could you describe the changes in your body and mind when you are companied by cats and dogs?

Ⅲ. Point of View.

To what extent do you agree with the main statement in the passage? Please talk about your thought and give some reasons.

Compare and Contrast

Ⅰ. Presentation.

Physical and mental health are equally indispensable for people. With the development of the society, more and more people have realized the importance of mental health. What are the differences of people's attitudes towards mental illness and what measures will people take at home and abroad? Please make a presentation in class based on the questions.

Ⅱ. Comment.

What do you think of Chinese traditional medicine and Western medicine? Please talk about your understanding after searching for relevant information through the internet and make some comment.

参考译文

第一单元

Text A
论游览

林语堂 著 越裔 译

[1] 旅行在从前是行乐之一，但现在已变成一种实业。旅行在现代，确已比在一百年前便利了不少。政府和所设的旅行机关，已尽力下了一番功夫以提倡旅行；结果是现代的人大概都比前几代的人多旅行了一些。不过旅行到了现代，似乎已是一种没落的艺术。我们如要了解何以谓之旅行，我们必须先能辨别其实不能算是旅行的各种虚假旅行。

[2] 第一种虚假旅行，即旅行以求心胸的改进。这种心胸的改进，现在似乎已行之过度；我很疑惑一个人的心胸，是不是能够这般容易地改进。无论如何，俱乐部和演讲会对此的成绩都未见得良好。但我们既然这样专心于改进我们的心胸，则我们至少须在闲暇的日子，让我们的心胸放一天假，休息一下子。这种对旅行的不正确的概念，产生了现代的导游者的组织。这是我所认为无事忙者令人最难忍受的讨厌东西。当我们走过一个广场或铜像时，他们硬叫我们去听他讲述某人生于1772年4月23日，死于1852年12月2日等。成年人在导游的指引之下，也变成了学童，而有许多比较好学不倦的人，竟还会拿着铅笔和日记簿速记下来。

[3] 第二种虚假的旅行，即为了谈话资料而旅行，以便事后可以夸说。我曾在杭州名泉和名茶的产地虎跑，看见过旅行者将自己持杯饮茶时的姿势摄入照片。拿一张在虎跑品茶的照片给朋友看，当然是一件很风雅的事情，所怕的就是他将重视照片，而忘却了茶味。这种事情很易使人的心胸受到束缚，尤其是自带照相机的人，如我们在巴黎或伦敦的游览事中所见者。他们的时间和注意力已完全消耗于拍摄照片之中，以致反而无暇去细看各种景物了。这种照片固然可供他们在空闲的时候慢慢地阅看，但如此的照片，世界各处哪里买不到，又何必巴巴地费了许多事特地自己跑去拍摄

呢？这类历史的名胜，渐渐成为夸说资料，而不是游览资料。一个人所到的地方越多，他所记忆者也越丰富，因而可以夸说得也越多。这种寻求学问的驱策，使人在旅行时不能不于一日中，求能看到最可能的多数的名胜地。他手里拿着一张游览地点程序表，到过一处，即用铅笔划去一个名字。我疑心这类旅行家在假期中，也是讲究效能的。

4 这种愚拙的旅行，当然产生了第三种的虚伪旅行家：即预定了游览程序的旅行家。他们在事先早已能算定将在奥京或罗京耽搁多少时候。他们都在起程之前，先预定下游览的程序，临时如上课一般地切实遵时而行。他们正好似在家时一般，在旅行时也是受月份牌和时钟的指挥的。

5 我主张真正的旅行动机，应完全和这些相反。第一，旅行的真正动机应为旅行以求忘其身之所在，或较为诗意的说法，旅行以求忘却一切。凡是一个人，不论阶级比他高者对他的感想怎样，但在自己的家中，总是唯我独尊的。同时他须受种种俗尚、规则、习惯和责任的束缚。一个银行家总不能做到叫别人当他是一个寻常人看待，而忘却自己是一个银行家。因此在我看来，旅行的真正理由实是在于变换所处的社会，使他人拿他当一个寻常人看待。介绍信于一个人作商业旅行时，是一件有用之物，但商业旅行是在本质上不能置于旅行之列的。一个人倘若在旅行时带着介绍信，他便难于期望恢复他的自由人类的本来面目，也难于期望显出他于人造的地位之外的人类天然地位。我们应知道一个人到了一处陌生地方时，除了受朋友的招待和介绍到同等阶级的社会去周旋的舒适外，还有比这更好的，由一个童子领着到深山丛林里去自由游览的享受。他有机会去享受在餐馆里做手势点一道熏鸡，或向一个东京警察做手势问道的乐趣。得过这种旅行经验的人，至少在回到家里后，可以不必如平时一样一味地依赖他的车夫和贴身侍者了。

6 一个真正的旅行家必是一个流浪者，经历着流浪者的快乐、诱惑和探险意念。旅行必须是流浪式的，否则便不成其为旅行。旅行的要点于无责任、无定时、无来往信札、无嚅嚅好问的邻人、无来客和无目的地。一个好的旅行家绝不知道他往哪里去，更好的甚至不知道从何处而来。他甚至忘却了自己的姓名。屠隆曾在他所著的《冥廖子游》中很透彻地阐明这一点。他在某处陌生的地方并无一个朋友，但恰如某女尼所说："无所特善视者，尽善视普世人也。"没有特别的朋友，就是人尽可友，他普爱世人，所以就处身于其中，领略他们的可爱处和他们的习俗。这种好处是坐着游览汽车看古迹的旅行家所无从领略的。因为他们只有在旅馆里边和从本国同来的游伴谈谈天的机会。英国人到了上海之后必住到英国人所开设的旅馆里边去，在早餐时照常吃着火腿煎蛋和涂着橘皮酱的面包，闲时在小饮室里坐坐，遇到有人邀他坐一次人力车时，必很羞涩地拒绝。他们当然是极讲究卫生的，但又何必到上海去呢？如此的旅行家，绝没有和当地的人士在精神上融合的机会。因此也就丧失了一种旅行中最大的益处。流浪精神使人能在旅行中和大自然更加接近。所以这一类旅行家每喜欢到阒无人迹的山中去，以便可以幽然享受和大自然融合之乐。

7 我以为除此以外，另有一种旅行，不为看什么事物，也不为看什么人的旅行，而所看的不过是松鼠、麝鼠、土拨鼠、云和树。观看景物和观看虚无，有极大的区别。有许多特去观看景物的，其实并没有看到什么景物，但有许多去观看虚无的倒反而能看到许多事物。所以我们须回到"旅行在于看得见物事的能力之哲学问题”，这就可使到远处去旅行和下午在田间闲步之间，失去它们的区别。

8 依金圣叹之说，两者是相同的。旅行者所必需的行具就是如他在著名的剧曲《西厢记》的评语中所说：“胸中的一副别才，眉下的一副别眼。”其要点在于此人是否有易觉的心和能见之眼。倘若他没有这两种能力，即使跑到山里去，也是白费时间和金钱。在另一方面，倘若他有这两种能力，则不必到山里去，即坐在家里远望，或步行田间去观察一片行云、一只狗、一道竹篱或一棵树，也能同样享受到旅行的快乐的。

（本文节选自：《生活的艺术》第十一章第一节）

Text B

我居于何处，又因何而生

亨利·戴维·梭罗　著

仲泽　译

1 切记，要学会让自己重新觉醒并保持清醒，不要采取机械手段，而要心怀对黎明的无限向往，即便沉入酣睡，这种黎明的光彩也不会弃绝我们。着意为之以求生命升华，生而为人，这是不容置疑的禀赋，我不知道还有什么比这更鼓舞人心。精确地绘画和雕刻，因此创作些许精致优美的作品诚然不错，但是，如果雕琢出一种氛围，描摹出一种方式，让我们借以审视，付诸践履，这才是瑰美有加的作品；让时光升华，这才是境界最高的艺术。每个人都身负使命雕琢生活，以使它值得我们在极为崇高，也无比光辉的时刻沉思默想，谛视品味，纵使每个瞬间和点滴亦复如此。如果我们弃绝既有的琐碎见识，或已将这些见识清理干净，诸神就会无比清楚地给我们启示，指导我们如何有效地行动。

2 我走近丛林，是因为我想带着明确的目的去生活，以图直面生命的本质，以验证我能否领会它蕴含的启示，以免在弥留之际，发现自己并没有真正活过。我无意过那种缺乏意义的生活——生活何其美妙！我也无意顺从天命，除非非常必要。我想深切地活着，吸纳生命所有的精髓，活得像斯巴达人那样刚毅强劲，以彻底革除并非生命本质的一切；披荆斩棘、斩草除根式地开拓出一条道路，将生命逼入死角，滤去其他，只剩下最基本的要素。如果生命注定卑琐，便彻底地掘出劣根公之于众；如果生命注定崇高，则用自己的经历予以印证，能让它在我下次的游历中得以显现。因为在我看来，绝大多数人对此生疏无知，将信将疑，他们都程度不同地得出草率的结论，“永远彰显主的荣耀，永远享受他的赐予”乃是今生的要旨。

3 经由神话得知，我们变成人类由来已久。虽然如此，我们却依旧生如蝼蚁，卑贱如故，浑似跟仙鹤打斗的俾格米人。如此生活，可谓补丁累叠，错上加错，尽管拥有智识，反倒因之奢侈不检而处境可悲，徒然将生命浪掷于鸡零狗碎之中。诚朴的人计点的数目很少超过他的十个手指，实在不得已，或许会加上十个脚趾，其余则会笼统视之。简约，简约，还是简约！告诉你，让事情剩下三件两件，而非成百上千；何须操心百万，半打足矣，将账目记在拇指盖上即可。在文明生活波涛汹涌的中心，人们得领受阴云、风暴、流沙的洗礼，考虑琐细繁多的事务，他若无法溺水沉没，全程也不想进避风港，就只能靠航位推测法保全性命，如果最终获得成功，便绝对是个计算高手。简单些，再简单些！为什么要一日三餐，如果可能就只吃一顿；为什么要杯盘碟盏放满桌子，五个够了，其他事情也相应地简化。我们的生活跟弹丸之邦杂凑而成的德国一样，其边界永远在变，连德国人自己也搞不清某一刻的疆界划分是什么情况。这个国家，就算将其所为的内务改革考虑在内——什么“内务”，顺便说一下，都是些浮皮潦草的“外务”——无非一个笨拙畸形的组织，因叠床架屋而弄得跋前疐后，且因虑事不周、鼠目寸光而毁于浪费奢华，跟遍及全国的千家万户没两样。疗救的唯一良方是厉行节约，追求高远，生活简朴乃至苛刻甚于斯巴达人。我们实在过于紧张，难得放松，人们觉得国家该有商业，该出口冰块，该使用电报，该一小时奔上三十英里（1英里约为1.6千米），且不管是否必要，他们却认为不可或缺而不加怀疑，至于我们应该生活得像人，还是像狒狒，他们倒捉摸不定。如果我们不加工枕木，铸造铁轨，也不日夜相继地做工，而只是对生活做点修补以求完善，还有谁愿意修筑铁路？如果没有修建铁路，我们怎能及时步入天堂？但是，如果我们待在家里沉浸于自己的事情，又有谁需要铁路？不是我们跨在铁路上，而是铁路跨在我们身上。你可曾想过铁轨下方的枕木都是什么？每一根都是一个人，不是一个爱尔兰人，就是一个美国人，铁轨压在他们身上，他们埋身于黄沙之中，火车就在他们身上疾驰。我敢说，他们睡得很死，每隔几年，就有一批倒在下面，任由机车狂驰而过。因此，如果有人在铁轨上奔驰而享受乐趣，另外有人就会遭受碾压而沦入不幸。当他们驶过一个梦中的漫游者——一根摆错了位置的多余枕木，而把他弄醒，他们就会突然停车，好似遭遇意外那般吵嚷抱怨。我欣然得知，就有一帮家伙被招在一起，每五英里安置一个，以保证那些“沉睡者”躺在原位，因为上述迹象表明他们可能会随时苏醒。

4 让我们像大自然那样从容度过每一天，在前行的途中，不要因纤芥之微而改变初衷；让我们早早起床，用或不用早餐，都优雅从容而无丝毫不安；任熙熙攘攘，人来人往，由钟声鸣响，孩子哭喊，决意过好每一天。我们为何要随波逐流，让步屈从？我们切勿处身日中的浅滩，而为一种名之为正餐的可怕旋涡和激流弄得忐忑不安、张皇失措。经历这些艰险后，你就会安然无恙，因为前面都是大道坦途。毫不松懈，满怀朝气，像尤利西斯那样缚身桅杆，去寻找另一条道路远航。如果火车的汽笛响了，就让它响吧，直到声嘶力竭。如果车站的铃声响了，我们为什么要跑起来？我们该做出判断那到底是什么音乐。观念、偏见、传统、幻觉和表象的泥淖遍及世界，从巴黎到伦敦，从纽约到波士顿到康科德，从教堂到政府，从诗歌到哲学到宗教，无处不在，无所不有。让我们镇定下来，行动起来，将双脚坚实地踏入那片泥潭，直到发现一块地方，那里有岩石和坚实的底部，那就是我们可以称之为真实的所在，然后可以说，没错，就在这里。有了这样一个基点，我们就可以居于洪流、寒冰和烈火的下方，在这里建一处墙垣或一个邦国，或稳妥地放置一个灯杆，竖立一个标杆，那并非尼罗河上的标尺，而是真实世界的圭臬，如此，后世才能知道，假象和幻景屡屡泛起的洪流到底有多深。如果你端庄正立，直面逼真的事实，就会看到太阳的两面都在放光，好似一把月形的东方短刀，在它将你从心脏到髓脑分作两半的时候，感受那华美的锋刃，此时，你就会欣然结束尘世的旅程。不管是生是死，我们只求真实，如果我们正在弥留之际，那就谛听喉头急促的喘息，感受大限将至的幽冷；如果我们活着，好，那就继续我们的事业。

5 时间只是由我们垂钓的一条溪流，我也在其中汲水取饮，但是，当我饮水的时候，却发现了它的沙底，也探得它是何其之浅。那纤纤细流逝去了，留下的却是永恒。我想去更深处取饮，想垂钓于天穹，它的底部是宛若卵石的繁星，我无法数得清楚，那里字母表上第一个是什么我也全然不知。我常常感到惋惜，为什么自己不像初生之时富于智慧。智识是一位刀客，他会洞见万物的隐秘，从中犀利地辟出一条道路。我再也不愿一无必要地让自己的双手忙碌，我的头颅就是手足，我感受到自己最卓越的官能都集中在那里。直觉告诉我，我的头颅就是用以开掘的利器，正如有些生命使用前爪和长吻，我会用它在这些山丘间掘进以开辟自己的道路。我想，最丰厚的矿脉就在这附近，凭着神杖和丝丝升腾的蒸气，我做出了判断：就从这里掘进。

（本文节选自：《瓦尔登湖》第二章）

第二单元

Text A

集体主义及其对当代中国社会的影响

肯德拉·彻丽

1 集体主义文化强调群体整体的需求和目标，而不是每个人的需求和愿望。在这种文化中，个人身份中发挥核心作用的是与群体中其他成员的关系以及人与人之间的相互联系。

2 集体主义与个人需求优先的个人主义形成对比。在集体主义文化中，如若人们慷慨、乐于助人、可靠并关注他人的需求，就会被认为是“好人”。这与个人主义文化形成鲜明对比，后者往往更注重自信和独立等特征。

3 集体主义文化的共同特征包括：

- 个人以与他人的关系定义自我（例如，“我是……的成员”）。
- 沟通往往更为间接，以避免潜在的冲突或尴尬。
- 鼓励团队忠诚度。
- 决策基于对团队最有利的事物做出。
- 做决定时往往折中，以达到更大程度的和谐。
- 团队合作和支持他人至关重要。

● 更强调共同目标而不是个人追求。

● 家庭和团体的权利先于个人的权利。

4 集体主义强调团体的重要性，而个人主义则注重每个人的权利和问题。在集体主义文化中，团结、无私或利他主义是重要的特征，而个人主义文化则倡导独立和个人身份。

5 这些文化差异是普遍存在的，可以影响社会运转的许多方面。例如，生活在集体主义文化中的人可能会为了集体的更大利益而牺牲自己的幸福。相反，那些来自个人主义文化的人可能会觉得自己的幸福和目标更重要。

6 个人主义文化中的人可能会用性格特质和特点来描述自己（例如，“我很聪明、有趣、热爱运动和善良”），但集体主义文化的人更可能会用他们的社会关系和角色来形容自己（例如：“我是一个好父母、好兄妹和好朋友”）。

7 研究表明，集体主义文化与低社会关系流动性相关联，这一术语描述了一个社会中个人有多少机会与自己选择的人建立社会关系。低社会关系流动性意味着人们的社会关系稳定、牢固且持久，其社会关系通常由家庭和地理区域等因素形成，与个人选择无关。

8 在集体主义文化中，与陌生人建立关系更困难，部分原因是结识陌生人通常更困难。陌生人在集体主义文化中比在个人主义文化中更易成为陌路人。矛盾的是，这意味着个人主义文化中的人会付出更多的努力和精力来积极维护亲密关系，通常需要通过增加自我表露和亲近行为等方式实现。

9 集体主义文化以稳定的关系为期待，与集体主义文化不同，个人主义文化中的关系往往更令人担忧和更脆弱。人们必须付出更大的努力来维护这些关系。在集体主义文化中，保持人际关系的和谐至关重要，这很可能是因为这些关系极难改变，不能保持和谐就意味着所有相关人员将会长期不快。

10 文化差异也会影响脱颖而出或融入团队成员的动机，某些行业更易墨守成规。根据发表在《经济增长杂志》上的研究，工业化前农业群体的后代倾向于集体主义文化，他们多从事更常规的而非创新性的职业。

11 集体文化有一些潜在的缺点。研究表明，集体主义文化可能会培养社交沉默和孤僻行为。集体主义文化中的人在与朋友分享个人问题时往往更加谨慎。研究表明，他们在工作场所分享知识时也很谨慎（即使是在团队中工作时），通常只有在受到激励或高度利他的情况下才会乐于分享。相反，人们往往寻求所谓的隐性社会支持。这包括花时间与支持自己的人在一起，而不是真正敞开心扉或解决压力的来源。

12 群体比个人更重要的观念在中国社会中非常普遍。为了理解中国集体主义对当代社会的影响，首先要考察这个概念的历史和起源。集体主义长期以来一直是中国文化的一部分，其根源可以追溯到公元前 5 世纪孔子的学说。根据儒家哲学，个人应该努力坚持和谐、孝顺和尊重权威的价值观。

13 集体主义的影响在当今中国社会随处可见。集体主义观念对经济和社会发展以及中国人民的价值观和信仰产生了深远影响。集体主义已经在中国文化中根深蒂固，并继续影响着中国人的思维和行为方式。

[14] 儒家思想在塑造中国人民的集体价值观和信仰方面发挥了重要作用。儒家强调家庭和集体的重要性，并鼓励个人优先考虑群体的需求而不是自己的需求。这种对集体价值观的强调帮助中国人民产生了强烈的忠诚度和凝聚力。

[15] 集体主义的概念也与中国传统的家庭结构密切相关。家庭是中国社会的基石，被认为是个人获得支持和指导的主要来源。家庭成员应共同努力实现他们的目标，他们高度强调团结的重要性。这种对集体责任的关注造就了家庭成员强烈的归属感和忠诚度。

[16] 集体主义对中国的经济增长产生了不可否认的影响。集体主义的概念鼓励个人共同努力实现共同目标，从而提高了生产力和效率。商业公司受到集体主义的极大影响，注重团队合作和协作成为成功的关键。此外，对集体责任的强调使企业家能够创建成功的企业。

[17] 集体主义也对中国企业家精神产生了积极影响。企业家被鼓励共同努力实现目标，集体责任得以强调，企业家能够创造成功的企业。这使得中国成为世界领先的经济体之一，拥有蓬勃发展的创业文化。

[18] 集体主义也对中国的社会稳定产生了重大影响。集体主义的理念鼓励个人共同努力维护和平与和谐，强调集体责任使政府能够实施有效的政策。此外，儒家传统价值观有助于培养中国人民的团结意识。

[19] 政府在促进社会稳定方面也发挥了重要作用。政府政策侧重于维护秩序和稳定，并鼓励个人共同努力实现共同目标。这产生了强烈的民族认同感和自豪感，有助于促进社会凝聚力和稳定。

[20] 事实证明，集体主义是一个对中国文化产生重大影响的重要概念。集体主义使中国人民能够一起努力实现共同目标，并有助于培养中国人民的团结意识。集体主义对中国文化产生了深远影响，并继续影响着中国人民的价值观、信仰和行为。

Text B

个人主义：根深蒂固的美国哲学

帕特里克·卡罗尔、丹·桑切斯

[1] 个人主义融入了美国文化。例如，我们重视独立性、创造力和自我表达。我们钦佩那些从人群中脱颖而出的人，他们个性独特、才能超群。我们奖励成就卓越的人，为英雄而欢呼。

[2] 但个人主义到底是什么，它如何融入美国传统？个人主义是一种哲学，它首先将人视为独特的个体，而不是群体的成员。它强调独立、个性和自主的重要性。

[3] 纵观历史，尤其是美国历史，许多人都体现了个人主义精神。这些人之所以脱颖而出，是因为他们去了其他人从未去过的地方，即使这需要极大的勇气。

[4] 美国最早体现这种精神的人是西欧探险家，他们在 15、16 和 17 世纪定居新大陆。与绝大多

数同胞不同，这些探险家愿意离开家园，在新生的殖民地为自己创造新的生活。当然，北美的生活并不轻松。他们面临着无数的困难，如疾病、寒冷和饥荒。然而，尽管如此，能够制定自己路线的希望推动了他们前进。尽管面临种种挑战，但新世界为他们提供了旧世界根本无法比拟的东西：一个建立新社会的机会。

5 到了 18 世纪，早期探险家的个人主义精神已经演变成了一种成熟的文化。然后，由于思想更加独立，殖民者坚持从英国获得相当程度的自治权。当乔治三世国王拒绝授予他们这种自治权时，美国革命就在《独立宣言》的鼓动下诞生了，这是一个名副其实的个人主义宣言。

6 革命带来了一个新的国家：美利坚合众国。尽管建国之父创建的政府体系有很多缺陷，但它植根于政治个人主义哲学，体现了人们按照自己认为合适的方式生活的权利。

7 当 18 世纪迈进 19 世纪时，新一代个人主义者大胆地向西部冒险，进入了边疆以外的未开发地区。面对严峻的条件和巨大的不确定性，这些“先驱”坚定而坚韧，抱着一种自力更生的态度，这就是后来的“粗犷的个人主义”。

8 作为个人主义社会发展中的关键人物，19 世纪美国哲学家拉尔夫·沃尔多·爱默生（Ralph Waldo Emerson）和亨利·戴维·梭罗（Henry David Thoreau）等在作品中探索并颂扬了这种自力更生。

9 但是，美国个人主义的历史并没有就此止步。事实上，随着对美国最后一个领域的探索，其他类型的探险家、先驱和革命者开始涌现，如发明家和企业家。

10 这个时期最著名的企业家之一是亨利·福特（Henry Ford）。福特出生于 1863 年，是一位非常有才华和成功的商人，这在很大程度上是因为他的创新理念。他通过引入流水线和大规模生产，使汽车产业发生了革命性变化，即使中下阶层也能买得起汽车。

11 但福特并不是唯一一个做出大胆改变的人。此时另一位知名人物是美国发明家和商人托马斯·爱迪生（Thomas Edison）。爱迪生以发明留声机、灯泡和许多其他产品而闻名，他还于 1882 年在纽约市创立了第一家由投资者拥有的电力公司。与福特和同时代的许多其他发明家一样，爱迪生的好奇心、创造力和创新思维帮助创造了许多我们现在认为理所当然的技术。事实上，从莱特兄弟（the Wright brothers）到亚历山大·格雷厄姆·贝尔（Alexander Graham Bell）和无数其他人，几乎所有当时的伟大发明家都愿意站出来探索新思想。

12 除了技术和科学，还有许多其他人在艺术、体育和道德引导等跨文化领域脱颖而出，鲍勃·迪伦（Bob Dylan）和约翰·列侬（John Lennon），还有马丁·路德·金（Martin Luther King Jr.）和理查德·费曼（Richard Feynman）。尽管这些人有着截然不同的故事和影响，但他们有一个共同点，那就是他们都与众不同。事实上，正是他们的独特性、差异性和个性使他们做出了他们所创造的影响力。

13 最近的革新者包括嘎嘎夫人（Lady Gaga）、约翰尼·德普（Johnny Depp）、戴夫·夏佩尔（Dave Chapelle）、乔·罗根（Joe Rogan）、埃隆·马斯克（Elon Musk）和史蒂夫·乔布斯（Steve

Jobs）。乔布斯本人不仅是个人主义者，他还将个人主义融入了苹果公司的品牌中。那些与众不同的人对他特别感兴趣。苹果 1997—2002 年推出的“非同凡想”广告宣传活动，就以上述众多标志性人物为特色，很好地体现了这一理念。宣传活动的电视广告词对此进行了说明。

14 “致疯狂的人。他们特立独行。他们桀骜不驯。他们惹是生非。他们格格不入。他们用与众不同的眼光看待事物。他们不喜欢墨守成规。他们也不愿安于现状。你可以认同他们，反对他们，颂扬或是诋毁他们。但唯独不能漠视他们。因为他们改变了寻常事物。他们推动人类向前迈进。或许他们是别人眼里的疯子，但他们却是我们眼中的天才。因为只有那些疯狂到以为自己能够改变世界的人，才能真正改变世界。”

15 从早期定居者到今天的领导者，许多人确实改变了世界。但他们引发的改变从来都不是通过墨守成规来实现的，改变总因他们的与众不同而出现。

16 个人主义不仅对文化产生了巨大影响，而且对社会理论，特别是政治哲学也产生了巨大影响。自由主义原则最著名的编纂见于《独立宣言》。

17 “我们认为这些真理不言自明，人人生而平等，造物主赋予他们某些不可剥夺的权利，其中包括生命、自由和追求幸福。”

18 托马斯·杰斐逊（Thomas Jefferson）及其合著者在制定《独立宣言》时，主要借鉴了被称为自由主义之父的约翰·洛克（John Locke）的哲学。洛克在《政府论下篇》中认为，个人权利是自由社会的基础，首先是自主权。根据这一基础，洛克得出结论，侵犯他人的财产权是错误的。

19 “自然状态有一种为人人所应遵守的自然法对它起着支配作用；而理性，也就是自然法，教导着有意遵从理性的全人类：人们既然都是平等和独立的，任何人就不得侵害他人的生命、健康、自由或财产。”

20 洛克说，政府由公民建立，“为共同维护他们的生命权、自由权和财产权，即俗称的私有财产”。

21 令人遗憾的是，将人视为个人的转变并没有像应有的那样迅速。尽管美国建国文件中所信奉的理想是崇高的，但早期的美国人却不愿意始终如一地运用这些理想。特别是种族主义和性别歧视政策仍然普遍存在，法律需要几十年才能承认妇女和黑人与其他人一样平等。然而，随着奴隶制、吉姆·克劳法、女性法律上受压迫等等级制度的废除，美国已经离实现其个人主义的建国原则更近了。希望这一进展能够为今后进一步保护个人权利提供启发。

22 一代又一代的革新者和开拓者更新和改善了我们的世界。随着时间的推移，新的创新者有机会站起来有所作为。通过下定决心制定自己的路线，我们也可以在一个停滞不前的世界中成为振兴变革的力量。我们可以在别人没有走过的地方开辟新的道路，我们可以为我们的后代人树立榜样。今天，大胆探索未知领域的机会比以往任何时候都更加真实。唯一的问题是我们是否会抓住它。你会吗？

第三单元

Text A

什么是“好孩子”？——在变化中的中国养育孩子

许 晶

1 2011年，耶鲁大学法学教授蔡美儿（Amy Chua）出版了她的回忆录《虎妈战歌》（*Battle Hymn of the Tiger Mother*）。所谓的亚洲育儿方式——包括严厉的管教、频繁的羞辱、甚至体罚，一切只为了一心一意地追求学业上的成功——成为美国主流媒体的热门话题。

2 不出所料，蔡美儿的书很快就被翻译成中文——但有一个有趣的转折。蔡美儿最初引人注目的书名被简简单单地命名为《在美国当妈妈》。更令人惊讶的是，这本回忆录在太平洋彼岸颇受冷遇。许多读过这本书的中国母亲说，蔡美儿的育儿方式与她们的经历完全没有共鸣。如果有的话，她们发现“虎妈”的方式即便算不得怪异，也相当令人不快。

3 “虎妈”的原型利用并强化了西方长期以来对中国人的刻板印象，但其中许多刻板印象早就过时了。这种变化是如何发生的？在21世纪的中国，做一个好孩子意味着什么？如果不是严格的服从，那么今天的中国父母希望他们的孩子做什么呢？

4 早在20世纪90年代初，人类学家吴耀辉（David Y.H. Wu）对上海家庭的教育方式进行了调查，他发现培养听话的孩子仍然是最重要的。一个好孩子就是一个听话的孩子，吴认为这是受多种因素影响的结果。一方面，他认为父母注重管教，因为人们普遍担忧“被宠坏的”这一代独生子女的未来。另一方面，他在其中看到了他所说的中国“威权主义、集体主义和民族主义”文化的影响。

5 然而，20年后，出现了一个非常不同的育儿景观。当被问及他们最看重孩子的什么道德品质时，41%的父母认为是“社交能力”，其次是“心地善良和关爱他人”“独立自主”。“顺从听话”是最不受欢迎的选择：只有2%的父母说这是孩子需要学习的最重要的品质。

6 这些结果表明，在中国，关于什么是好孩子的观念正在发生变化。尽管对被宠坏的独生子女的担忧从未消失，但严加管束的方法——在学术界被称为“威权式教育”——已经在国内失宠。相反，自2010年代初以来，中国父母一直试图向孩子灌输良好的社会行为和独立意识。

7 这个过程不应该被理解为向所谓的西方、个人主义的养育方式的线性发展。的确，“西方”育儿方法已经被重新包装，并以权威和科学的形象兜售给了城市中产阶级消费者。这些强调孩子自主性和社会情商的书籍也的确塑造了中国人的育儿价值观。但中国父母并不盲目地吸收或追随西方模式。他们会谨慎地评估这些观念，并将它们与自己的情况进行比较。

8 例如，中国父母希望培养出更善于交际的孩子，并不仅仅是因为他们希望模仿西方的育儿方式；这至少在一定程度上是由于人们越来越不相信学习成绩是孩子未来的唯一决定因素。近年来，随着学校和就业市场的竞争日益激烈，许多中国人开始相信，学历不再足以区分求职者，人际交往能力越来越被视为孩子未来成功的重要指标。

[9] 与此同时，培养更强独立性的愿望与担心独生子女被宠坏有关，这种同样的担忧曾导致父母走上对孩子严加管束的道路。特别是，许多年轻父母表达了他们的焦虑，认为他们的孩子受到了太多的庇护，他们的内心变得太脆弱了。因此，独立有了新的含义：它不是不服从的标志，而是自力更生和心理上富有韧性的标志。考虑到父母们看到下一代面临的激烈竞争和挑战，这种韧性尤其值得称赞。

[10] 然而，如果家长对好孩子的理解正在改变，那么许多学校对好学生的定义仍然停留在过去。年轻的父母希望培养孩子的独立性或保持他们的创造力，在面对仍然以顺从和服从为优先的教育方式时，往往不得不妥协自己的理想。

[11] 比如，一位母亲就对幼儿园喜欢表演精心编排的舞蹈表示了担忧。她三岁儿子的班级花了一个月的时间排练儿童节的舞蹈。她抱怨说，“他们是孩子，不是运动员”。“我希望看到他们自然自发地做事情，我认为这可能比完美无瑕的集体舞蹈更好看。在集体舞蹈中，每个孩子都必须按照老师告诉他们的方式移动。这就像一场机器人表演。”

[12] 学校系统并不是当今父母们面临的唯一严峻现实。许多父母发现，在一个仍然非常重视获胜的社会大环境中，培养孩子的道德品质尤其困难。父母们认为孩子应该是天真无邪的，表现他们“天生”的美德和善良，不被成人世界的虚伪和诡计所污染。然而，他们也担心心思单纯、真诚善良的孩子会不适应他们将来会步入的真实社会。

[13] 这一现实有助于解释一个看似矛盾的现象：虽然个别中国父母可能会拒绝“虎妈”的教育方式，但在过去十年里，他们让孩子参加了越来越繁重的课业和培训课程。在最极端的例子中，一个5岁的孩子在一个周末参加了8个课外班。但这场军备竞赛的动机并不一定是内在的。相反，许多父母感到不得不逼迫他们的孩子，即使他们担心培养一个好孩子并不总是等同于培养一个好学生。我们需要了解中国人如何在世界上竞争最激烈的教育环境中应对困境和挑战，而不是诉诸便利的文化刻板印象。

[14] 在今天的中国，无论你是在大城市还是在农村的县城，关于如何培养一个“好”孩子的焦虑是很普遍的。中国父母很少想把自己看作专制的“虎妈”，但他们也知道，被庇护的猫咪可没法在现实世界生存。

（本文作者许晶，华盛顿大学人类学系附属助理教授，美国教育科学院博士后研究员。她的研究着眼于当代中国的儿童发展、教育、家庭和道德。她是《培养好孩子：道德与儿童发展》一书的作者。）

Text B

过度养育的父母和新一代美国儿童

瑞安·蔡

[1] 过去十年，在美国出现了一种日益增长的趋势：过度养育。更具体地说，这是美国人对美国

儿童的过度养育，而它正反映在决策和法律判决中，这让老一辈人摇头。尽管存在代沟，但越来越多的证据和研究已经开始揭示这一趋势的一个令人不安的影响，应该引起真正的关注。这种过度养育的父母，以及由于对孩子过度养育的态度而盛行的做法，极有可能培养出这样一代年轻美国人，他们高度厌恶风险、胆小怕事、没有准备好成为关心社会的公民和积极活跃的领导人。

2 过度养育指的是父母对孩子采取的一系列行为，这些行为共同起作用，以防止孩子冒任何有损其情绪或身体健康的风险。庇护，不断的监督和事无巨细的管理，防止承担责任，过度迎合和过度安慰，控制社交范围，过度谨慎都是可识别的行为，可以被认为是过度养育计划的一部分。很多人会发现，就算不是全部，也对这些行为中的大部分都非常熟悉，这只不过是因为它们在今天的对话中已经变得更加常见，在我们自己的个人生活中也可以观察到。

3 至于出现这种趋势的原因，在于以下几个同时出现的趋势，它们不仅表明过度养育的趋势愈演愈烈，而且能帮助我们理解我们可能面临的未来。

不断恶化的信任感

4 美国人不再那么信任彼此了。一项基于 1972 年至 2012 年综合社会调查（GSS）汇编的数据分析显示，认为大多数人可以信任的美国人的比例从 1972 年的约 46% 下降到 2012 年的约 32%。按代际划分，数据还显示，从婴儿潮一代[1]到千禧一代[2]，信任程度显著下降。在“老一代”中，40% 到 50% 的人认为大多数人都是可以信任的，而只有 25% 的 X 一代[3]和只有 19% 的千禧一代对同一问题给出了肯定的答案。

5 这种差异的部分原因可能是由于不同的世代处于不同的人生阶段，但这种差异足以表明，这种信任的丧失与父母过度保护的增加有关。当美国人开始减少彼此的信任时，特别是已经为人父母的千禧一代，他们开始对孩子施加更多的限制，更多的监督，以免别人影响他们的孩子。他们不让孩子在社区闲逛，控制孩子与其他孩子和成年人的交往。

技术

6 过去十年的科技进步极大地推动了我们在养育子女方面所看到的变化。现在，孩子无聊的时候父母不再送他们出去，而是选择给他们电子设备让他们玩儿。这种变化是好是坏并不在过度养育这一话题范围之内，但它确实说明了父母过度养育是多么容易。在全球定位系统跟踪和智能手机的时代，每时每刻都盯着孩子变得很容易，而几个小时不联系孩子则更难。

媒体和互联性

7 当被问及为什么父母会过度养育时，为什么许多人会归咎于媒体呢？答案是：更紧密的互联

1 指二战结束后，1946 年初至 1964 年底出生的人。

2 指出生于 20 世纪时未成年，在跨入 21 世纪（2000 年）以后达到成年年龄的一代人。

3 指出生于 20 世纪 60 年代中期至 70 年代末的一代人。

性。由于科技的发展，更强的互联性似乎是一些父母试图保护孩子远离危险的根源。由于能够接触到来自全国各地的新闻和信息，人们很容易陷入一个陷阱，认为在国家的另一边发生的事情也很容易发生在你所在的地方。它滋生了一种危险和风险持续存在的错觉，弊大于利。

更高的养育期待

8 与本讨论相关的最后一个趋势是，父母的养育期待已经发生了文化上的转变。如今的文化鼓励父母们过度养育，更多地控制孩子的教育和未来。当科学和进步似乎正在解决与人类生活条件有关的所有问题和风险时，为什么父母不能采取同样的科学养育方法控制养育环境来给孩子提供一个安全、快乐的生活呢？对于越来越多的父母来说，这并非不可想象。这是必要的，也是合乎道德的。

过度养育的影响

9 所有这些同时出现的趋势结合在一起，形成了这样一种形象，那就是：与前几代人相比，今天的养育方式为什么和怎样在过度养育程度上是独一无二。但是过度养育意味着什么呢？

10 有些人会说，今天的养育方式造就了更好的父母，更成功的孩子，并帮助父母更多地参与到孩子的生活中。因此，有些人会认为，这不是一种过度养育的趋势，更准确地说，这是一种建立更好的亲子关系的趋势。

11 然而，研究和数据证明情况并非如此。尽管有些父母的初衷是好的，但科技和其他促成因素使父母很容易过多地参与到孩子的生活中，并在这么做的时候对孩子的生活进行干预和控制。父母可以轻易地做这些事情，因而也就做得更加频繁。

12 至于过度养育对孩子健康的影响，研究表明，过度养育会导致孩子规避风险，依赖父母，面临更高的心理疾病风险，缺乏强有力的应对机制，出现慢性焦虑。一个不被允许去冒险或自主做选择的孩子，在不得不面对一个混乱世界的严酷现实时，必然会面临很多焦虑和麻烦。有趣的是，过度养育的影响与疏于管教的影响有着惊人的相似之处，尽管程度较轻。

13 总而言之，孩子们会更少具备成年人那种应对世界压力的能力。与十年前相比，大学生患严重精神疾病的比例更高，服用精神疾病药物的学生比例也更高。在校园咨询中心对数百名专业人士的采访显示，“缺乏应对技能正是当今大学生的特点所在”。如今的年青一代通常也更有可能认为自己承受的压力比老一代多。这些差异部分可以归因于年轻人没有像老一辈那样学会如何应对压力，但也有部分原因在于，孩子们被送进大学，却没有在他们生活的早期通过独立思考和冒险来掌握必要的自我管理技能。

14 作为一国国民，我们必须问问自己，我们想成为什么样的国民。依靠父母和国家养活自己的国民，或者为周围人的利益做出贡献的国民。我们养育子女和受到的养育方式往往反映了我们如何看待世界和我们作为公民的行为方式。把过度养育当成美国养育方式的一个标志，无异于迈向一个人们只知索求不愿付出的社会。父母应该对孩子的克服困难、承担风险和独立能力有更多的信心。

只有这样，我们才能重振乐观主义和精神，而这个国家今天似乎已经失去了这种乐观主义和精神，而且现在非常需要这种精神。

（本文改编自：https://bprberkeley.edu/2019/4/16）

第四单元

Text A

中国减贫创造了世界奇迹

丛培武

1 在我 2019 年来加拿大任职之前，曾有不少朋友向我推荐位于大兴安岭山麓的一座小城——阿尔山，他们认为那里景色十分优美，堪比落基山脉中的班夫，非常值得一看。遗憾的是，由于准备工作紧张，我未能成行。

2 抵加后，出于好奇心，我查阅了一些关于阿尔山的材料，发觉这座小城的确不同寻常。那里有美丽的湖泊、森林、雪山，还有广阔的草原和世界上最大的温泉群。与班夫不同的是，直到 2011 年，阿尔山还是中国国家级的重点贫困县，不仅没有游客，当地人的温饱都成问题。在国家旅游扶贫战略的帮助下，那里的旅游业快速发展，走出了“旅游 + 扶贫”带动贫困人口稳定脱贫的希望之路，2018 年旅游收入 52.7 亿元人民币（约 8.13 亿美元），较 2013 年增长 280%，2019 年阿尔山正式退出中国国家级贫困县行列。

3 阿尔山的成功只是中国减贫奇迹的一个缩影。中国政府 70 多年间成功实现 8.5 亿人摆脱贫困。仅改革开放 40 多年来，中国就有 7.5 亿人脱贫。特别是中共十八大以来，中国政府把脱贫攻坚摆在治国理政的突出位置，组织实施了人类历史上规模最大、力度最强的脱贫攻坚战。自 2012 年起，中国每年减贫规模都在 1 000 万人以上，相当于欧洲一个中等国家的人口规模。2020 年 11 月，中国如期完成新时代脱贫目标，832 个贫困县全部脱贫摘帽，消除了绝对贫困和区域性整体贫困，提前 10 年实现联合国 2030 年可持续发展议程的减贫目标。

4 中国减贫的关键特点是把“精准扶贫”作为扶贫开发的基本方略，对不同贫困人口分别制定不同的脱贫方案，通过发展生产、易地搬迁、生态补偿、发展教育、社会保障兜底等实现脱贫。中国还实施电商扶贫、旅游扶贫、光伏扶贫等“十大扶贫工程”。在上述政策带动下，中国减贫成效覆盖包括少数民族在内的广大人群。截至 2019 年年底，新疆累计脱贫人口达 292.32 万人。西藏 74 个贫困县全部“摘帽”，人均纯收入从 2015 年年底的 1 499 元增加到 2019 年的 9 328 元，历史性消除了绝对贫困。作为中国少数民族人口最多的省份，广西实现 54 个贫困县全部“摘帽”，境内的壮族人口整体脱贫。

5 中国的脱贫攻坚为全球减贫事业做出了重要贡献。作为世界上减贫人口最多的国家，中国对全球减贫贡献率超过 70%。中国设立了“中国 – 联合国和平与发展基金”和“南南合作援助基金”，并在“东亚减贫合作倡议”“中非减贫惠民合作计划”框架下扎实推进合作项目。中国在非洲援建了 24 个农业技术示范中心，惠及 50 多万当地民众。

6 消除贫困是人类面临的共同挑战，也是 2030 年可持续发展议程的首要目标。据联合国开发计划署数据，受新冠疫情影响，2030 年极端贫困总人数将超过 10 亿，实现全球减贫目标更加任重道远。中国和加拿大在消除贫困、促进男女平等、应对气候变化等方面有很多共同语言。追求美好生活是中加两国人民的共同愿望，我们可以携手努力，为国际减贫事业、为人类更光明的未来做出更大贡献。

（Adapted from: http://ca.china-embassy.gov.cn/xw/202102/t20210209_10321240.htm）

Text B

据报道，去年美国新增 100 万名百万富翁，最富有的人变得更富有

罗伯特 · 弗兰克

1 新报告称，去年的股市繁荣和加密货币升值在美国新创造出 100 多万个百万富翁。

2 财富调研公司斯佩特兰集团的报告指出，2021 年，可投资资产超百万美元的美国人数量从 2020 年的 1 330 万人飙升至创纪录的 1 460 万人。

3 超 10% 的百万富翁增长率是近年来最高的，这得益于股市、加密货币和其他资产创造的数万亿美元财富。

4 斯佩特兰集团的主席乔治 · 瓦尔波说：“这是各领域百万富翁最高产的一年。”

5 顶级富豪的增长是最迅猛的。身家超 2 500 万美元的美国人数量暴增了 18%。身家超 2 500 万美元的美国人数量从 2020 年的 21.4 万人达到了现在破纪录的 25.2 万人。相比之下，财富在 10 万美元到 100 万美元之间的所谓的“大众富豪”投资者数量只增长了约 2%。

6 迄今为止股市是 2021 年百万富翁和其他富豪财富增长的最大驱动力。标准普尔 500 指数去年增长了 27%，而纳斯达克指数增长了 21%。美联储数据显示，2021 年最富有的 1% 美国人的股市财富增长了超 3 万亿美元。

7 加密货币和其他资产也增值了，包括非同质化代币、收藏品和房地产，这让富人的财富进一步增加。币虎（CoinGecko）数据显示，尽管价格波动很大，但去年加密资产的总市值增加了 1.5 万亿美元，达到了逾 2.3 万亿美元。

8 私募股权和风险资本的投资也大幅升值。因为富人有更多钱可用于投资，尤其是那些高风险高回报的投资，所以 2021 年超级富豪的投资收益也比大众富豪更多。

9 瓦尔波说：“富人可以广泛涉猎各种投资。去年不只是传统的流动性市场表现出色，另类投资、房地产投资和加密货币的收益也不错。”

10 顶级富豪财富的增长也扩大了美国的贫富差距。美联储的数据显示，最富有的 1% 美国人拥有的财富在去年增长至创纪录的 32%。

11 财富专家指出，考虑到通胀率暴涨、利率上升和可能发生的经济衰退，2022 年或将无法保持去年的财富涨幅。今年以来股市下跌已经开始令投资者的利益受损。迄今为止纳斯达克指数已下跌了 14.5%，标准普尔指数下跌了 8.4%。

12 沃尔波（Walper）说："每一天都在变化，所以难以预测今年的财富走向如何。但是 2022 年开局的前几个月已经描绘出与 2021 年不同的图景。"

13 全球最富有 26 人的财富总和相当于最贫穷的 38 亿人的财富总和，慈善机构牛津饥荒救济委员会（Oxfam）发布了这份关于财富严重不平均的报告。报告称自 2008 年全球金融危机以来，全球亿万富豪的人数翻倍。并且他们的财富每年增加 25 亿美元。这与全球最贫困之人形成了鲜明的对比——随着商品价格增长、工资紧缩以及土地和房租价格上涨，世界上最贫穷之人眼看着他们的财富慢慢缩水。Oxfam 的报告强调了不断增长的世界贫富差距以及日益扩大的财富分配不均。

14 报告表示世界上大部分超级富豪都是从科技公司，如亚马逊、微软以及脸书中赚得他们巨大的财富。世界首富是亚马逊创始人兼 CEO 杰夫 · 贝索斯。他所拥有的 1 000 亿美元财富是埃塞俄比亚年度健康预算的 100 倍。Oxfam 表示是时候尝试纠正财富不平衡了。其建议征税收入水平更加公平化，对个人收入以及公司利润征收更多的税并消除公司和超级富豪常用的避税计划。其表示："在很多国家，体面的教育或有质量的医疗保健成了只有富人才能供得起的奢侈品。"

(Adapted from: https://www.cnbc.com/2022/03/17/million-new-millionaires-were-created-in-us-last-year-report-says.html and https://breakingnewsenglish.com/1901/190123-wealth-inequality.html)

第五单元

Text A

孔子与《论语》

赖蕴慧

1 春秋时期，社会动荡不安，孔子（公元前 551– 公元前 479 年）因此提出社会伦理道德改革，他的建议中包括消除当权者的权力滥用和剥削行为。这一进程将由贤能者发起和领导，他们具有渊博的知识，并具有道德洞察力，是大家的榜样。作为这些思想的倡导者，孔子常常被认为是儒家学说的创始人（儒家学说在西方被称为儒家传统）。儒家，那些饱学之士，积极倡导并努力实现其主张，即实现国家治理伦理道德。从历史上看，儒家是士大夫运动的部分产物，会被任命为当权者的顾问。儒家教育在于教化人们实现一种有道德和有礼仪的有序生活。一些儒家将严格的宫廷礼仪扩展到社会和家庭活动。由于这种现象，儒家有时被认为是崇尚传统宫廷礼仪行为的传统主义者。有趣的是，在《论语》7：1中，孔子指出他只是传播者，而不是创造者。

[2] 实际上，《论语》的篇章并不是出自孔子之手，而是由他的弟子和再传弟子编纂而成。幸存的文本可能在西汉时期成为正式文本。最近，学者们也将注意力转向了另一个出土的版本，比先前广为接受的版本要早。

[3]《论语》共499章，编排并不系统，重复和前后不一致的现象屡见不鲜。因为由许多作者撰写而成，所以人们对《论语》中的关键概念有几种不同的解读。可以看出，反映孔子思想的篇章与后人修改或插入的其他篇章有所差异。我们也可以将《论语》的文本视为更全面地了解儒家思想史和中国思想史的来源。因此很多当代学者——尤其是哲学家——把《论语》看作开放式的文本。这些学者继续研究对《论语》文本的新评论和其思想在当代的应用。在阅读《论语》时，我们可以感受到孔子是一位忠诚、尽责和成熟的思想家。在许多篇章中，上自君主，下至村夫，都曾就善政以及美好生活的问题向他咨询。这些篇章讲述了孔子如何考虑平衡各种因素以做出决定。许多第一次阅读《论语》的读者会感到震惊，因为孔子的决定缺乏基本规范原则或标准。例如，在《论语》13：18中，他希望儿子和父亲互相掩盖彼此的罪行：

> 叶公语孔子曰："吾党有直躬者，其父攘羊，而子证之。"孔子曰："吾党之直者异于是。父为子隐，子为父隐，直在其中矣。"

[4]《论语》13：18通常被认为是不道德的，因为它赞成说谎。一些人很难理解孔子，一个家喻户晓的儒家伦理的创始人，怎么会提出这样不道德的建议？但如果我们继续反思这段文字，我们会有更多问题。比如：如果有惩罚，对盗窃的处罚是什么？一只羊的价值是多少？邻居会受到怎样的影响？如果孩子揭露父亲的盗窃行为，会对孩子造成什么结果？如果他不这样做，后果又是什么？这个孩子的情况尤其特殊，并没有简单的解决方案。推测这些问题的"正确"答案是徒劳的。我们应该关注更相关的问题，例如家庭和忠诚在伦理生活中的地位，关系的伦理意义，为他人掩饰的必要条件，孔子的道德伦理考虑方法及其标准。

[5] 实际上，孔子要对君主说的治国之道，或者孔子在吃饭时如何就座，对我们今天来说意义不大。也许我们不应该期望《论语》能够为我们的伦理困境提供规范的答案。相反，我们可能会通过阅读《论语》，来了解早期儒家所理解的道德理性中相关的复杂性。如果这是正确的，我们可能会了解儒家是如何研究古代文本的（论语8：8；1：15；7：18；8：3），并从过去启蒙者的经验中学习（《论语》7：22）。从这个角度来看，《论语》是记录他人行为的典籍，而不是一本权威语录集，也不是一部全面系统的哲学论著。作为规范行动和行为的指南，《论语》可使我们对自己的行动和承诺进行反思性思考。

[6] 以此方法，我们来审视一番儒家思想中的一个基本概念"仁"。与"礼"相同，"仁"凝聚了儒家人文主义的理想。对儒家哲学的任何理解都取决于我们如何理解这两个基本概念以及它们之间的相互作用。

仁

7 “仁”在孔子之前的文本中偶尔提及。在其早期的用法中，该词指的是某种男子气概或男子气概的品质，尤其是君主的品质。例如，在《诗经》的两首狩猎诗中，“仁”指两个“英俊并仁”的猎手（施瓦茨，1985：51）。在《史记》(《尚书》)中，“仁”是指统治者对臣民的仁慈态度。然而，在儒家的传播中，“仁”逐渐开始表示人类的道德品质特征。因此，在早期儒家哲学中发现它的不同也就不足为奇了，它表示一般的人性，是人性的一个显著特征，或人类美德。这一特征以多种方式被提及，但最常见的是与生俱来的性格或集体社会政治生活的特征。这个概念的含义也体现在它的汉字中：“仁”由两个字符组成，左边是人，右边是二。这表明该概念与人类休戚相关。因此，这个词被翻译成不同的英文，如仁慈、爱、仁性、仁道、仁德、怜悯和同情。《论语》中“仁”的含义是多方面的，近来的翻译中避免用某个英语单词来将其等同。

（本文节选自：赖蕴慧著作《中国哲学概论：剑桥哲学概论丛书》第 2 章）

Text B

苏格拉底的道歉

1 雅典人啊，为了赢得一点点时间，你们会因此而招致恶名，遭受那些诋毁这个城市的人的指控，因为你们杀死了苏格拉底，一个有智慧的人。要知道，攻击你们的时候会说我是聪明人，虽然实际上我并不聪明。只需要再等一些时间，你们所希望的事自然就会发生。你们看，我已这把年纪，死期不远了。我说这些是讲给想判我死刑的人听，对于他们我还有话要说。

2 雅典人啊，也许你们认为我是因为不会说话，因为对你们进行了一番规劝才被定罪的；如果我按照你们认为合适的方式做所该做的，说所该说的，这样我就会被释放。不是的！老实说，我并不是无话可说，我只是不愿厚颜无耻，拣你们爱听的话来说罢了。你们想让我哭哭啼啼，苦苦哀求，去说有损我人格的话——这种话在别处听来虽然早已司空见惯。虽然我命在旦夕，但我不会做那些屡见不鲜、低贱卑微的事。对于我的辩护我也毫不后悔，我宁愿为我说话的方式而死，也不愿以你们爱听的方式做辩护而生。不管是在法庭还是在战场，一个人都不应该为了逃生而不择手段。在战场上，毫无疑问，如果向敌人缴械投降，下跪求饶，他将免除一死。在其他危急情况下，也有其他免死的办法，只要他愿意去说某种话或者去做某件事。同胞们，死里逃生并不难，难的是逃避罪恶，而这往往比死亡来得快。如今我年事已高，行动迟缓，就逃不过死亡了。然而那些控告我的人机灵，跑得快，那跑得快的罪恶就抓住他们。你们判了我死刑，我即将离去，而他们也将被真理判为不义的恶徒。我接受对我的惩罚，你们接受对你们的惩罚。我想这些都可以被看作命吧，本该如此，没有什么不好的。

3 让我们换种方式来证明吧，我此去极有机会得福，因为死后只有两种可能：一种是死后真的就一了百了，死者再无一切知觉；另一种正如人们所说，死后灵魂就从这个世界跑到了另一个世界。假设死后是一种无知觉的状态，就像是在睡觉，而且连梦也没有，这样看来，死了倒是一种妙不可言的收获。我想，假如让一个人挑选他安然无梦的一夜，去和他其他的日夜相比，让他说说有多少日日夜夜有这一夜舒服，我敢说，任何人，且不说哪一个人，即便是国王，也找不出几个日夜比这一夜更舒服。既然死是这样的性质，那死就是件有益的事情，因为死后，一个晚上也就成了永恒。从另一方面看，如果死真的是灵魂从一个地方换到了另一个地方，正如人们所说，我的朋友们啊，所有的死者都到那里去，还有什么比这更幸福的事吗？一个人来到那个世界，离开这儿的法官，并被送到另一个世界真正的法官那里，如弥诺斯、拉达曼托斯、埃阿科斯、特里普托勒谟斯以及其他英雄，他们生前都是大公无私的人物，我们迁居到那里岂不是求之不得吗？而且能遇见俄耳普斯、穆赛俄斯、赫西俄德、荷马，有谁会不愿意呢？这如果是真的，我愿意死千万次。在那个地方，能够与帕拉墨得斯和忒拉蒙的儿子埃阿斯，以及其他早年间因遭错判而致死的人交谈，那将有无穷的乐趣。把我的遭遇与他们的比较一番，那生活真是妙不可言。最痛快的是，我可以继续像在这个世界一样，探索真理和谬论。去发现他们中哪些人是聪明的，哪些是自以为聪明而并不聪明的。陪审员们，当你们能够去研究率领大军攻打特洛伊的统帅，研究奥德修斯、西绪福斯以及其他无数说得出的男男女女，怎么会划不来呢？能够和那些人相处、交谈，真是有无穷的乐趣和享受。在那个世界，如果所说的全部属实的话，是绝不会因此就将人处死的。在其他方面，他们也比在这个世界的人要幸福得多，而且他们是永远不会死的。因此，陪审员们，对于死，我们应乐观看待。你们知道事实上祸事是不会降临在好人身上的，不论在他生前还是死后。神灵不会对他以及他的所有置之不理的。我将面临的死亡也不是自然的生老病死，只是我看得很清楚，死亡和因此带来的解脱对我而言是更好的选择。因此神也没有给出任何干涉我的暗示。这也是为什么我对那些控告我的人和将我判罪的人都不感到愤怒的原因。然而，正因为如此，我并不责怪判我有罪的人，责怪指控我的人。而他们却认为这样做会伤害到我。对这一点，他们着实应当受到指责。

[4] 我还有一个要求，等我的几个儿子成年以后，如果他们追求的是金钱，注重别的什么胜过道德的东西，或者他们自以为是，其实并不行，那么就请你们像惩罚我那样惩罚他们。要是他们不关心他们应该关心的事情，成天想着自己是怎样的人，事实上却什么也不是，那就请你们像我指责你们一样，去指责他们。你们如果这样做，我和我的儿子们就算得到了公正的对待。离开的时辰到了，我们各自走我们自己的路——我死去，你们将活下来。谁的命运更好，没有人知道。

（本文节选自：柏拉图的《苏格拉底的道歉》，托马斯·G. 韦斯特编写，康奈尔大学出版社出版）

第六单元

Text A

中国饮食趋势：一切向好

1 中国健康消费者越来越受到关注。随着收入的增长和受教育程度的提高，中国人开始更加关注健康和保健，这在饮食方面尤其明显。鉴于饮食和营养在保持健康过程中举足轻重的地位，我们决定调查中国人饮食习惯的主要发展趋势。我们发现，这个过去饱受饮食问题困扰的国家，现在更加注重健康，并且正在积极调整自身的饮食。

2 饮食和健康与人口和经济变化趋势密切相关。中国的健康和保健发展趋势大多与其不断增长的收入和更加富裕的中产阶级密不可分。瑞信报告称，2015 年中国的中产阶级群体为 1.09 亿人，比美国还多。与此同时，麦肯锡预测，到 2020 年，中国的中产阶级规模将达到 4 亿人。其中一半是中上阶层，年收入相当于 16 500～35 000 美元。中国向以中产阶级为主的社会转型本身构成了一股极其强大的社会力量，对饮食和健康产生了相应的影响。

3 随着 20 世纪 80 年代中国的改革开放及经济繁荣，人们收入增加，越来越多的人搬到城市并加入了中产阶级行列。随之而来，传统上健康、以素食为主的饮食习惯发生了转变，人们开始食用更多肉类、乳制品、盐、脂肪和糖。这种饮食变化对健康产生了极大的负面影响。

4 然而，随着收入的持续增长和人们受教育程度的提高，许多人现在开始更加关注于改善他们的健康。健康意识提升的人口比例必定会在未来几年中继续保持增长。

肥胖和糖尿病处于临界水平

5 中国目前面临由不良饮食习惯引起的一系列重大健康问题。

6 中国是世界上肥胖人群数量最多的国家，约有 12% 的成年人被归为肥胖，30% 的人超重。甚至在儿童群体中，也有近 10% 的人超重，6% 的人肥胖。这意味着如果不采取有力措施来改变现状，中国未来的健康问题就会像定时炸弹一样，随时可能爆发。

7 早在 20 世纪 80 年代，当中国大多数人保持简单的传统饮食习惯时，糖尿病只影响了 1% 的人口。随着收入的快速增长和不健康饮食习惯的形成，糖尿病发病率已经飙升到人口的 11%。2015 年中国有 1.09 亿糖尿病患者，占所有受该病困扰人数的三分之一，预计到 2040 年，这一数字将增加到 1.5 亿。除此之外，目前估计有近 5 亿中国人处于糖尿病前期。

8 财务成本巨大。中国大约 13% 的医疗费用被认为与糖尿病有关，据估计，到 2030 年，这一数字将达到 470 亿美元。

快餐口味变化快

9 中国见证了快餐消费的繁荣期。2011 年，肯德基的母公司百胜集团宣布，其 18 亿美元的全球利润中有一半来自中国。肯德基目前在全国拥有 6 000 多家门店，2017 年的收入为 50 亿美元。麦当劳则正以每周 10 家门店的速度扩张。

10 然而，最近的趋势显示快餐消费的增长速度在显著放缓。随着中产阶级的饮食习惯变得更加理性，快餐已经失去了其吸引力。为了更好应对这一变化，快餐店正提供更健康的品类。例如，肯德基现在允许顾客在烘烤或油炸方式上自由选择。

11 尽管如此，预计 2019 年快餐销售额仅增长 2%，是整个餐饮服务业中增长最慢的部分。

快速增长的肉类消费放缓

12 自 20 世纪 80 年代以来，中国的肉类消费从大约 100 万吨猛增至 2010 年的 800 万吨以上。在 20 世纪 80 年代初期，中国人均每年食用肉类大约 13.6 千克。现在，这一数字已经飙升至每人每年 63.5 千克——然而，这仅为美国普通公民消费量的一半。

13 然而，最近来自荷兰合作银行的一份报告指出，由于消费行为的变化，中国肉类消费增长将显著放缓。

食糖消费合理，控盐迫在眉睫

14 就健康而言，糖是最重要的食品成分之一。然而它被认为是肥胖和糖尿病等健康问题的罪魁祸首，如上所述，这些疾病是当代中国的主要健康问题。然而中国的食糖消费量远低于全球平均水平。尽管在过去几十年里它的消费量确实有所增加，但糖并不是中国传统饮食的主要组成部分。据联合国粮农组织称，中国食糖消费存在地区差异，中国南方的消费水平最高，农村地区的消费水平低于城市地区。但最近的趋势显示农村地区食糖消费量有所增加，而城市地区食糖消费量则呈下降趋势。

15 过去几年，中国食糖消费增长疲软，预计 2018—2019 年将保持相对稳定。然而，全球食糖产量过剩已将价格推低，这可能会刺激更多的消费。尽管如此，由于健康安全的考虑和甜味剂替代品的使用，其长期趋势是平稳的。

16 虽然中国的食糖消费量远低于全球平均水平，但食盐消费量却恰恰相反。发表在《柳叶刀》上的一项研究报告称，中国的食盐消费量是世界上最高的。研究人员报告说，80% 的社区每天的平均钠摄入量超过 5 克，显著高于大多数其他国家每天 3～5 克的钠摄入量。中国的食盐消费量是世界卫生组织推荐水平的两倍，是美国居民平均消费量的两倍。这可能是大约三分之一的中国成年人患有高血压的重要原因，而高血压会导致心脏病和中风，在中国这是两大致命疾病。正因如此，就其对健康的负面影响和减少食盐消费的需求而言，食盐在中国的健康议程中是一个重要议题。

17 可喜的是，食盐的消费量呈下降趋势。这主要是由于饮食习惯的变化和食物冷藏方法的大量应用。联合国儿童基金会和中国官方食品安全机构的一项研究发现，2000 年至 2009—2011 年间，中国的食盐消费量下降了 22%。尽管如此，由于腌制蔬菜和酱油等调味料的大量消费，以及加工食品消费量的增加，钠摄入量在同一时期仅下降了 12%。

软饮料消费下降，酒类消费增加

18 太古饮料总经理帕特里克·希利（Patrick Healy）最近告诉《南华早报》，中国消费者越来越多地选择更健康的饮品。他提到他们正在拒绝经典软饮料，转而专注于高档饮用水和功能饮料。虽然传统软饮料将继续以个位数的速度增长，但他表示新兴的饮料产品将以两位数的百分比增长。欧晰析企业管理咨询公司（OC & C Strategy Consultants）的合伙人史蒂夫·夸克（Steven Kwok）预测低糖、无糖和低热量饮料未来“将成为主导”。

19 然而，酒类消费却呈上升趋势。虽然中国最受欢迎的白酒销量较 2017 年下降了 20%，但啤酒销量却增长了 31%。据报道，威士忌和葡萄酒的销售也在增长。据《柳叶刀》报道，中国高水平的酒精消费导致该国与酒精相关的死亡人数激增。这主要归因于男性饮酒人群，因为男性饮酒的人数是女性的三倍。事实上，酒精对中国女性健康的影响远低于世界平均水平。

挑战依然存在，未来一片光明

20 中国中产阶级作为全球消费主力，他们的饮食和消费趋势值得研究。我们的调查显示，在过去的几十年里，中国人的饮食状况恶化，肉类、快餐、糖和加工食品的消费量增加，这导致了肥胖、糖尿病、中风和心脏病方面的重大健康危机。然而，最近的饮食趋势显示，快餐、食盐、糖和软饮料的消费发生了积极变化。中国人越来越关心饮食的安全与健康，与健康关联的公司应致力于满足这些愿望。

（Adapted from: https://gocohospitality.com/chinese-diet-trends/）

Text B

美国饮食怎么了？

克里斯·伍尔斯顿

1 美国饮食怎么了？以下便是专家们的回答：“卡路里太多了”，正如纽约大学营养与食品研究教授、公共卫生硕士玛丽昂·奈索（Marion Nestle）博士所说。注册营养师、美国癌症研究所前营养教育主任梅拉妮·波尔克（Melanie Polk）也明确表示“卡路里太多了”。曾任美国饮食协会发言人的注册营养师芭芭拉·戈尔曼（Barbara Gollman）在自己的理论中也持“卡路里过多”的观点。

2 也许是时候停止谈论高脂肪食物，并承认我们只是摄入了过多的卡路里。25 年前，美国人平均每天消费大约 1 850 卡路里的热量。从那时起，我们的日常饮食已经增加了 304 卡路里（大约相当于两罐苏打水）。从理论上讲，这足以让每个人每年多增加 31 磅（约 14 千克）。从持续的肥胖流行来看，许多美国人正经历体重增加——而且会继续增加。

3 以最新的全国体重调查为例。根据疾病控制和预防中心的数据，超过 68% 的美国人被认为超重或肥胖。（这意味着他们的体重指数大于 25。）

4 但卡路里并不能说明一切。要真正了解美国饮食存在什么问题，就必须知道我们是如何摄入所有这些卡路里的。有两种可能的极端方式：吃大量高热量食物，或者饮食过量，许多人两者兼而有之。我们对快餐的喜爱产生了特别严重的恶果。尽管联邦政府建议我们每天至少吃两到五杯水果和蔬菜，但调查显示，美国人平均每天只吃三份，42% 的人每天吃不到两份。

5 下面仔细看看我们对卡路里的热爱——以及它所带来的健康危机。

哈哈镜

6 当然，没有统一的美国饮食模式。我们都有各自的品位、怪癖和习惯。但专家们还是通过我们的食物选择总结出了清晰的规律。事实上，大多数美国人的饮食模式不外乎两类："西方的"或"节制的"。

7 节制的饮食是营养师的梦想。这类饮食模式的人通常吃鱼、家禽、十字花科蔬菜（卷心菜和西兰花）、绿色蔬菜、西红柿、豆类、新鲜水果和全谷物较多。 他们很少吃脂肪或高热量的食物，如红肉、鸡蛋、高脂肪乳制品、炸薯条、比萨饼、蛋黄酱、糖果和甜点。

8 西方饮食像通过哈哈镜看健康饮食一样，一切都是相反的：红肉和其他高脂肪食物排在前列，而水果、蔬菜和全谷物则被置于一边。除了脂肪和卡路里，西方饮食还富含胆固醇、盐和糖。如果这还不够糟糕的话，它还严重缺乏膳食纤维和许多营养素——以及有助于保护心脏和抵御癌症的植物性物质（植物化学物质）。

9 把它们放在一起无异于一场灾难。发表在《内科医学档案》上的一项针对 69 000 多名女性的为期 12 年的研究，发现西方饮食会显著增加患冠心病的风险。其他研究表明，高脂肪、低营养的饮食会增加患结肠癌、糖尿病和许多其他疾病的可能性。

分量扭曲

10 西方饮食并不陌生。比起现在，20 世纪 50 年代典型的美国家庭吃猪排和土豆泥的可能性远大于炒豆腐和西兰花。那么，为什么肥胖流行病在过去 20 年中暴发了呢？这是个数量问题。戈尔曼表示："20 年前，人们的饮食不像今天这么多样化，人们吃的水果和蔬菜也不够多，但这些更符合人们真正的需求。"

11 从百吉饼店到家庭餐厅，从自动售货机到电影院特许摊位，再到餐桌，我们的餐点和小吃占据了很大比例。雀巢指出，"食品行业都认为他们必须增加分量以保持竞争力，人们很快就习惯了大分量，因此现在正常分量看起来却很轻薄。"

12 饮食过量在外出就餐时尤为明显。波尔克说："透过任何一家大型连锁餐厅的橱窗，你都会看到大盘的食物从厨房里被端出来。"任何一盘食物都可以很轻松地提供 2 000 卡路里的热量，这足以让大多数人吃一整天。

便利文化

13 尽管全国都痴迷于减肥，但肥胖流行病仍然是一个全国性的健康问题。人类对脂肪和甜食的渴望永远不会消失，而现在满足这些渴望变得比以往任何时候都容易。全国有 170 000 家快餐店和 300 万台软饮料自动售货机，大剂量的卡路里总是触手可及——尤其是当这些汽水零售机就设立在公立学校时。

14 例如，《快餐国家》作者埃里克·施洛瑟（Eric Schlosser）称，1978 年，美国青少年正常每天喝大约 7 盎司（1 盎司约为 28.3 克）苏打水。如今，这一饮用量几乎是原来的三倍，每天高达 9% 的卡路里来自苏打水。同龄女孩则紧随其后。

15 也许不足为奇的是，研究表明，儿童肥胖在过去几十年中已达到流行病的程度。据专家介绍，罪魁祸首是：高脂肪食物、苏打水和运动不足。

节制

16 肥胖、不平衡和过量可以用来概括美国饮食的特点。但这不一定是你的饮食模式。"人们认为健康饮食是一项艰巨的任务，但细节可以决定成败，"波尔克说，"你只需采取一些有效的策略，比如自我管理。"

17 如果每周在外用餐超过四次，你可以从健康用餐开始做起。"随着我们在餐馆吃饭的次数越来越多，我们必须对那些稀奇古怪的饭菜进行挑选。"波尔克说。选择烘烤、蒸熟或烧烤类的食物，而不是油炸食物；把沙拉酱或其他脂肪配料作为配菜；直接跳过那些非低脂蛋黄酱；以沙拉和开胃菜代替主菜。如果确实点了主菜，预留至少一半打包回家。

18 无论你在哪里吃饭，都尽量遵守一些基本准则。你所需的量取决于自身的年龄和活动量——例如，十几岁的男孩和成年男性比幼儿吃得更多。目标是每天吃 3 ～ 8 盎司的面包、麦片、米饭或意大利面，全谷物越多越好。这并不像听起来那么令人生畏——一杯米饭算作 2 盎司，一片面包算作 1 盎司。每天两到五杯水果和蔬菜会给你提供纤维和重要的营养；如果你用的是盘子，尽量让农产品占据盘子的一半空间（一份是中等大小的水果、半杯切碎的水果、半杯切碎的蔬菜或一杯新鲜蔬菜）。水果、蔬菜和谷物加在一起可以充饥，同时在保证卡路里最低摄入量的基础上，为你的身体提供足够的能量。

19 可以吃肉，但试着把它看作是你膳食的补充，而不是主要的食物。根据美国农业部（USDA）提供的食物金字塔，你每天只需从"肉类组"中选择两份的量（最多 6 盎司半）。该组包括肉类、家禽、鱼、干豆、鸡蛋和坚果。当然，6 盎司的三文鱼、斑豆或鸡胸肉比六盎司的雪花牛排营养更丰富（顺便说一句，一份肉应该大约是一副纸牌的大小）。

20 许多建议可以归结为一个词：适度。通过从金字塔的每个部分吃不同的食物并控制分量，你可以让自己的饮食健康又营养。现在我们比以往任何时候都有更多的选择和诱惑，但我们对吃什么也有最终决定权。让我们控制饮食，享受生活吧。

（Adapted from: https://docslib.org/Whats-Wrong-With-The-American-Diet）

第七单元

Text A
故宫博物院

1 故宫博物院成立于 1925 年，建立在明朝（1368—1644）和清朝（1644—1911）皇宫的基础上。故宫（也被称为紫禁城）宏伟的建筑群，大量的书画、陶瓷以及皇家古董藏品使其成为中国和世界上最负盛名的博物馆之一。1961 年，国务院将故宫列为中国重点文物保护单位之一，1987 年联合国教科文组织将故宫列为世界遗产。

故宫博物院的位置和布局

2 故宫博物院坐落于北京市中心，由天安门进入，北边紧挨着景山，东边和西边则分别是王府井和中南海。中国古代的钦天监为故宫的位置赋予了宇宙意义。在他们看来，皇帝的住所是地球的轴心，北极星是天空的中心，于是便将二者联系起来。故宫由于其中心地位和出入限制，也被人称为紫禁城。明朝的第三位皇帝永乐皇帝于 1406 至 1420 年间建造了故宫。永乐皇帝篡位后，决定将首都从南京北迁至北京。200 多年后，明朝于 1644 年灭亡，清入关。1911 年，辛亥革命者推翻了清王朝。大清的最后一位皇帝溥仪退位后仍住在故宫内，直到 1924 年被驱逐出去。故宫历经近五百年的王朝统治，是 24 位皇帝的住所和朝堂。

3 紫禁城周围环绕着 10 米高的宫墙和一条 52 米宽的护城河。紫禁城的建筑群面积达 112 万平方米，从北到南共 961 米，从西到东共 753 米。紫禁城的四角各有一个大门。正门名午门，北门名神武门，东门名东华门，西门名西华门。游客们由午门进入，能看到一连串的殿堂沿着中轴线依次排开。故宫建筑庄严绚丽，泛黄的屋顶好似漂浮在朱红的墙壁之上，古老的彩绘屋脊和雕刻更是放大了这一宏伟的景观。

4 紫禁城的南部被称为外朝。外朝有三所大殿——太和殿、中和殿与保和殿。三所大殿的两侧分别为体仁阁和弘义阁。外朝是皇帝上朝接见大臣的场所。

5 与这一排列相呼应的是紫禁城北部的内廷。乾清宫、交泰殿和坤宁宫位于中轴线上，东西六宫位于中轴线两侧，是皇帝与后妃居住生活的地方。其他位于内廷的建筑包括东部的斋宫、诚肃殿，西部的养心殿、雨花阁和慈宁宫。内廷不仅是皇帝与妃嫔居住的场所，还是举行宗教仪式和行政活动的场所。内廷的最北端是御花园。

6 外朝和内廷的建筑总面积约为 16.3 万平方米。这些建筑严格按照传统的建筑等级规范设计，这一规范指定了具体特征，以反映皇帝的至高权威和地位。老百姓们不能也不敢靠近紫禁城。

故宫博物院的成立

7 1911 年的辛亥革命以末代皇帝溥仪退位而告终。临时政府允许溥仪继续居住在紫禁城的内廷当中。与此同时，1914 年，藏于热河（今河北省承德）与奉天（今辽宁省沈阳）的宫殿之中的皇家珍宝都被转移到紫禁城，在外朝进行公开展出。1924 年，军阀冯玉祥发动政变，溥仪最终被逐出紫禁城。皇宫的管理权归一个委员会所有，该委员会负责解决被废黜的皇室的相关事宜，以及审核皇家藏品。经过一年的不懈准备，1925 年 10 月 10 日，委员会在乾清宫前举办了盛大的仪式，标志着故宫博物院初步建成。1925 年出版的 28 卷目录显示，清朝皇室留下的珍宝数量超过 186 万件。所有珍宝均被分为不同的门类。展览厅也开放用以展示一些珍宝。

故宫博物院藏品的迁移

8 在二战爆发前不久，日本占领了中国东北，并继续向北京进军。威胁在即，博物院管理者决定撤离藏品，以免落入敌手或遭受战争侵害。在 1933 年 2 月至 5 月这一动荡时期，藏品中最重要的部分被打包成 13 427 个板条箱和 64 捆，分五批运往上海。1936 年，这些藏品被派往南京，南京建造了一座藏品馆，并成立了故宫博物院的一个分馆。

9 1937 年 7 月 7 日，卢沟桥战役的开始标志着抗日战争全面爆发。不到一年，日本人就入侵了中国东部的大部分地区。藏于南京的珍宝不得不再次通过三条路线转移到四川，藏匿于四川的巴县（今重庆巴南区）、峨眉和乐山。直到战争结束，这些珍宝才得以在重庆汇合，并于 1947 年返回南京。随着长江以南的共产党军队即将取得胜利，日渐疲弱的国民党开始向台湾撤退。从 1948 年底到 1949 年，国民党挑选了 2 972 箱货物通过海峡运往台中储存。这些箱子里的东西构成了台北故宫博物院的藏品。台北故宫博物院于 1965 年对外开放。虽然至今仍有 2 221 箱国宝留在南京，但南京保存的大部分国宝已逐渐归还北京。

10 在这动荡的战争与革命的十年里，尽管古董数量惊人，但没有一件藏品丢失或损坏。这在很大程度上要归功于故宫博物院工作人员坚定的意志，他们在保护这些宝藏方面取得了巨大的成绩。不幸的是，由于这场长期的动荡，一些藏品散落到了各种机构中。20 世纪 50 年代初，中华人民共和国成立后不久，故宫博物院的工作人员带着满满的决心和热情，要恢复故宫昔日的辉煌。博物馆管理部门启动了一项全面修复的政策。故宫内所有高的建筑都安装了避雷针，同时安装了现代系统用以防火和确保安全。此外，自 20 世纪 80 年代初开始实施改革以来，政府也一直将维护故宫周围的护城河作为优先事项。

故宫博物院的发展

11 尽管过去的紫禁城是一座密不透风的堡垒，但现在的故宫却是一座公共博物馆。故宫博物院藏品丰富，代表了 5 000 年的中华文明和 600 年的紫禁城历史。故宫博物院自 1925 年成立以来，经历了许多发展，并期待着将过去的遗产传承给后代。现在，故宫博物院一如既往地致力于保护国家遗产，并努力成为世界各地博物馆的典范。

Text B
白金汉宫

1 自 1837 年以来，白金汉宫一直是英国君主在伦敦的官方住所，如今也是英国君主的行政总部。尽管白金汉宫用于举办许多官方活动和国王的招待会，但每年夏天白金汉宫的国事厅都对游客开放。白金汉宫有 775 个房间，包括 19 间国事厅、52 间皇家卧室和客房、188 间员工卧室、92 间办公室和 78 间浴室。从尺寸上看，这座建筑的正面长 108 米，深 120 米（包括中庭），高 24 米。

白金汉宫的历史

2 乔治三世在 1761 年为妻子夏洛特女王购买了白金汉府邸，将其作为一个舒适的家庭住宅，靠近当时用于举行许多宫廷活动的圣詹姆斯宫。白金汉宫后来被称为女王之家，乔治三世的 15 个孩子中有 14 个出生在这里。乔治四世在他 1820 年登基时，决定把房子改造成一个临时居所，其用途与他父亲乔治三世使用时相同。随着工作的进展，到 1826 年底时，乔治四世改变了主意。在他的建筑师约翰·纳什（John Nash）的帮助下，他开始把房子改造成一座宫殿。议会同意 15 万英镑（1 英镑约为 8.7 万人民币）的预算，但国王要求 45 万英镑作为更实际可行的额度。纳什保留了主体结构，但在朝西的花园一侧增加了一套新的房间，使其面积增加了一倍。其外立面为色彩柔和的巴斯石灰石，体现了乔治四世对法国新古典主义的偏好。

3 经过改造的房间是国事厅和半国事厅，自纳什时代以来几乎没有改变。白金汉宫的南北两翼被拆除，并重建了一个更大规模的凯旋门——大理石拱门——作为一个扩大庭院的中心装饰，以纪念英国在特拉法尔加和滑铁卢战役的胜利。到 1829 年，花费已上升到近 50 万英镑。纳什的铺张浪费使他失去了工作。1830 年乔治四世去世时，他的弟弟威廉四世委托爱德华·布洛尔（Edward Blore）完成这项工作。这任国王从未搬进宫殿。事实上，当 1834 年国会大厦被大火烧毁时，国王提议将这座宫殿作为议会的新场所，但被拒绝了。

4 1837 年 7 月，维多利亚女王成为第一位入住白金汉宫的君主。1838 年 6 月，她也成为第一位从白金汉宫前往加冕典礼的英国君主。1840 年，她与阿尔伯特亲王结婚后，白金汉宫的缺点很快显示了出来。对这对新婚夫妇来说有一个严重的问题，那就是没有婴儿房，而且客人卧室也很少。唯一的解决办法是移动大理石拱门（现在位于海德公园的东北角），建造第四翼，从而形成一个四方形。新建厢房的费用主要来源于乔治四世将布莱顿的皇家凉亭出售的钱。布洛尔在宫殿的主体部分增加了一层阁楼，并在外部装饰了原本为纳什的大理石拱门设计的大理石饰条。这项工程于 1847 年完成。在世纪之交，由于伦敦臭名昭著的煤烟，布洛尔东线硬度低的法国石头显示出风化的迹象，需要进行更换。1913 年时，设计过众多大型公共建筑的阿斯顿·韦布爵士（Sir Aston Webb）受命为其做新设计，重新修缮其外观。韦伯选用了波特兰石，在动工之前花了 12 个月的时间来准备这些石料。当工程开始时，工匠又花了 13 周的时间来对石料进行重新打磨，这一过程包括移除旧的砌石。

5 现在的宫殿前院，也就是举行卫兵换岗的地方，形成于 1911 年，是维多利亚女王纪念碑方案的一部分。门和栏杆也是于 1911 年完成的；北中门现在是宫殿的日常入口，而中门用于国事场合，换岗后警卫也从中门离开。这项工程是在 1914 年第一次世界大战爆发之前完成的。

白金汉宫的现状

6 如今，白金汉宫主要是一座用于办公的建筑，也是英国君主立宪制的中心。它被用作举行各种王室活动和典礼，包括从招待外国元首到在授勋典礼和招待会上庆祝成就等。

7 白金汉宫每年都有超过 5 万人来访，主要在国宴、午宴、晚宴、招待会和游园会这些场合。国王也会每周在这里会见首相，并在白金汉宫接待新任命的外国大使。

8 白金汉宫全年都会举办各种招待会，以表彰工业、政府、慈善、体育、英联邦和其他生活领域的工作。比如在 2015 年时，女王就为橄榄球世界杯的球员、组织者和支持者举行了招待会。

9 白金汉宫经常是重大国家庆典和纪念活动的焦点。2002 年纪念女王登基 50 周年时，在白金汉宫花园举办了一场音乐会，布赖恩·梅（Brian May）在宫殿屋顶上演唱了令人难忘的《天佑女王》。2012 年女王登基 60 周年庆典时，公众们受邀在白金汉宫花园举行特别的野餐。

10 白金汉宫的阳台是世界上最著名的阳台之一。这个皇家阳台首次被记录是在 1851 年，当时维多利亚女王在庆祝世界博览会开幕时登上了它。从那时起，皇家阳台的亮相成为许多重大场合的标志，如女王每年的官方生日庆典、皇家阅兵仪式结束时观看皇家空军的飞行表演、皇家婚礼，以及不列颠之战 75 周年纪念日等具有国家意义的特殊事件。

11 虽然白金汉宫被视为王室的行政中心，但它也是一个家庭住宅，许多皇室婚礼也在白金汉宫举行，最近的一场是剑桥公爵和公爵夫人的婚礼。

12 给国王及其直系亲属日常活动和职责提供支持的办公室，如私人秘书办公室、女王私库办公室都位于白金汉宫。

第八单元

Text A

忙里抽暇顾健康

张雷（音译）

1 20世纪70年代，从阿特金斯（Atkins）饮食到斯卡斯代尔（Scarsdale）饮食，西方世界大力追求时尚饮食，数百万本相关书籍被售出，提振了出版界市场。大约在同一时间，朋克摇滚乐在世界范围内首次亮相。

2 50年前，饮食和朋克已无缝地结合在一起，流行在中国各地，给我们带来朋克饮食这一养生之道。

3 当然，时尚饮食值得注意的一点是，它们往往都有一个吸引人的名字，这个名字一般也会十分适合朋克饮食。事实上，严格来说，这个名字似乎描述了一种生活方式——甚至是一种态度——而不是一种饮食制度，即使它确实与一个人的饮食有关。此外，与中国的许多类似的新型现象一样，它的起源，或至少其名称，似乎是在网络空间中构思出来的。

4 但让我们暂时离开互联网，进入现实世界，谈谈如何识别朋克养生者。想想这样三幅画面：首先是一个年轻人一只手拿着一个热水瓶杯子，里面散发出蒸汽，另一只手拿着一个杯子，里面有半杯加冰的苏格兰威士忌。第二幅画面是一位熬到半夜还很精神的年轻女士，坐在那里敷着最昂贵的面膜。第三幅画面是三人来到迪斯科舞厅，打着健身的幌子，在跳舞的间隙喝着泡有枸杞的威士忌。

5 因此，不同于强调健康饮食和进行体育锻炼的传统饮食，21世纪出生的Z世代倡导的朋克饮食在两个极端之间来回跳跃，它的实践者不仅开心于其中的讽刺，而且对他们正在引领一种时尚的生活方式感到高兴。

6 然而，当你深入研究这一切的细微之处时，你会发现，年轻人似乎确实给自己施加了——或已经给自身施加了——如此沉重的学业和工作压力，难怪他们在年纪轻轻就已经意识到，他们最好也开始关心自己的健康状况。

7 去年，《国家健康观察报告》称，在20世纪60年代、20世纪70年代、20世纪80年代和20世纪90年代四个年龄组中，年龄越小，对个人健康的看法就越模糊。

8 江苏省东南大学附属中大医院心理精神科的蒋文秀说：“一方面是工作和生活节奏普遍加快，另一方面是对失去竞争优势的焦虑。”

9 “年轻人似乎总是觉得他们必须做些什么来保护自己的发际线，或者抵抗眼角上的细纹。”

10 市场咨询公司艾瑞咨询（iResearch）去年的一项调查发现，在熬夜的年轻人中，近42.6%的人通常在晚上10点到11点之间入睡，近33.7%的人通常在晚上11点到深夜12点之间入睡。其余的23.7%的人说，他们在午夜后睡觉，并且有与不规律工作和休息有关的长期问题。

11 70% 的晚睡者说他们一天可以睡七个小时，近 8% 的人说他们严重缺乏睡眠，平均睡眠时间不超过五个小时。此外，通过对比不同睡眠时间组，发现睡眠时间越早，深度睡眠的比例越高（7 小时或更长），睡眠时间越晚，严重睡眠剥夺的比例越高（5 小时或更短）。

12 蒋文秀说："在年轻的上班族中，在工作繁忙的时候狂饮咖啡几乎已成为家常便饭。他们琢磨着眼前的黑眼圈，下一秒你会看到他们把枸杞放入在日本买的保温壶里。"

13 蒋文秀轻松地总结了当代年轻人的养生之道："他们一生中有一半时间在透支健康，另一半时间在啜饮被赋予了所谓神奇功效的保健品。"

14 一直着眼于营销机会的医疗保健公司也发现了这种现象，比如有 351 年历史的北京同仁堂药店。它研发了一种被称为"中药咖啡"的产品来满足人们的需求，这种新产品的名字听起来像是一种保健品。

15 同仁堂本应果断投身到这一新兴的营销风口，其加入也与朋克饮食生活方式的讽刺性十分吻合，因为当人们想到同仁堂时，脑海中无疑会浮现出如下画面：古香古色的旧商店中陈列着产品，周围有雕刻的木梁和绘画，盛放药物的老式容器，还几乎总会有一位上了年纪、银发白须的中医。

16 同仁堂是中国最负盛名的传统药店之一，始建于 1669 年，即清朝康熙八年，自 1723 年开始致力于皇家医学，188 年来曾为八位皇帝提供过服务。

17 同仁堂销售的朋克非传统饮料包括：枸杞拿铁、开胃美式、益母草玫瑰拿铁、利尿消肿桂花蜜豆咖啡等等。

18 同仁堂咖啡店的咖啡师李胜利说："我们将枸杞软化、压制成浆，加入咖啡中。枸杞能够滋养肝脏和肾脏。对于经常熬夜的人来说，喝枸杞拿铁是个不错的选择。"

19 李胜利是一名有着多年经验的咖啡师，他说自今年在同仁堂工作后，他意识到自己可以从中医的角度认识咖啡。咖啡本身可以缓解疼痛，可与枸杞、橘皮和肉桂等中草药搭配，富含钾和抗氧化剂。

20 不过，草本咖啡只是同仁堂对年轻消费者加以关注的冰山一角。在北京朝阳区同仁堂知嘛健康一号店，一楼还提供养生汤、粥和糕点面包等包装零售产品；二楼是传统药店，可以挂号、咨询和销售药品。

21 负责品牌推广的苏晓航表示，草药咖啡不是营销的重点，但同仁堂希望用咖啡和快消产品吸引消费者，创建一个反映健康生活的新环境。

22 苏晓航在最近接受中新社采访时提道："通常情况下，一个人感到不适会去看医生、把脉、买药，然后回家。"

23 "我们计划强调药物和食物的同等重要性，并通过饮食疗法治愈人们。"

24 艾瑞研究公司最近关于年轻人健康消费趋势的报告发现，在 21 世纪出生的人中，超过 90% 的人普遍意识到健康的重要性，其中超过一半的人采取实际行动为自己做些事情。

25 当然，踏上追求健康之旅，首要之务便是配置健康的产品。一个遵循朋克养生并且经常加班的人可能会饮一瓶补气膏来恢复活力，嚼两块阿胶糕提亮暗淡的肤色，喝一杯速溶银耳羹滋润干燥的皮肤，或者吃几颗黑芝麻丸来护理那禁不住轻触的脆弱秀发。

26 最近，第一财经商业数据中心、阿里健康有限公司和天猫科技联合发布了一份名为《新食品主义》的报告。根据该报告，2018 年和 2019 年传统补品的销售额增长了 20% 以上，并且在过去三年中，20 世纪 90 年代出生的人已成为传统补品在线购买的主力军。

27 “我们一直认为保健品是老年人的市场，但随着人们经济状况的不断改善，年轻人对自身形象管理和身体健康的关注有助于针对年轻人的保健品的崛起。”北京工商大学营销学教授郭欣说。

28 根据市场研究公司欧睿国际的报告，中国医疗保健品行业去年营业额达 1 627 亿元，比 2018 年增长 9.8%。报告显示，国内保健品市场价值达 1 000 亿元人民币。分析人士表示，由于年轻人对健康重要性的认识不断提高，越来越多的公司正在进入这类市场。

Text B

失去触摸

——不曾拥抱的一年将如何影响心理健康

埃莉诺·摩根

1 狗能做到的事情不多，但也不少。我独自和员工住在一起，在第一次封锁的第八周，她开始盯着我那一直紧绷的手翻白眼。在宣布封锁之前，由于新冠肺炎及其后遗症，我一直赖在沙发上，就这样度过了春天和夏天，未曾和其他人有过实际意义的触摸。我怀念朋友衣服和侄子头发的味道，但最重要的是，我怀念只有人才能带来的地气儿。来自身体太阳神经丛的疼痛和这些想法混杂起来，常常让我措手不及。

2 对触觉的需求存在于意识的视界之下。出生前，胎儿被包围在子宫的羊水中，胎儿的神经系统可以区分自己和母亲的身体，彼时人对自我的全部概念植根于触觉。伦敦大学学院心理动力学神经科学教授卡特琳娜·福托普卢（Katerina Fotopoulou）博士认为：“人体基于看护者的触摸建立了所有模型。我们完全依赖看护者来满足身体的核心需求。没有接触几乎什么也做不到。”

3 今年 40 岁的尼娜·史密斯（Nina Smith）独自住在伦敦南部。她的脊柱在 2018 年受过伤，之后经历了漫长的恢复期，需要长时间卧床休息。虽然会有人来探望，但她的疼痛程度意味着很难进行触摸。尼娜自认为对如何准备第一次封锁有很好的预见性。“我原以为我知道结果会怎样，”她通过视频软件 Zoom 说道，“例如，我知道我必须严格遵守散步的日常作息；在不同的环境中散步，能够让人感觉稍微好一点。”但六周后，她的决心开始崩溃。“我经历过的孤独让我比想象中更脆弱。我试图让自己保持规律作息，但……”她开始哭泣。“在某种程度上，不能拥抱真的很痛苦。我认为政府没有考虑到第一次封锁对独居者的影响。”

4 作为成年人，我们可能无法理解触摸的重要性，即使在触摸消失了的情况下。利物浦约翰摩尔大学的神经学家、情感触碰领域的专家弗朗西斯·麦格隆（Francis McGlone）教授说："我们可能开始意识到缺少了什么，但并不会始终意识到缺失的是触碰。但当我们谈论孤独的问题时，我们往往忽略了显而易见的事实：孤独的人缺失的恰恰是抚摸。"

5 牛津大学进化心理学家罗宾·邓巴（Robin Dunbar）教授表示，触觉对我们的身心健康都有巨大影响，他说："与亲密的朋友和家人在一起时，我们彼此之间的接触比意识到的更多。"邓巴的研究发现，作为成年人，我们平均有五个可以依靠在他们的肩膀上哭泣的朋友。"我们在灵长类动物身上发现了完全相同的东西，"邓巴提及，"即使在规模更大的灵长类动物社会中，每一层级都会出现由五个最好的朋友组成的群体，聚在一起相互梳理毛发——这是它们的社交接触形式。在灵长类动物和人类中，这些紧密的联盟起到缓冲作用，能够让你远离世界上的烦恼。"2020年，有来自112个国家的40 000人参加了BBC和一家医疗主题博物馆联合开展的一项调查，最常用来描述触摸的三个词是："安慰"、"温暖" 和 "爱"——这并不是一个令人惊讶的结果。

6 随着疫情的持续，许多人将试图在没有抚摸的情况下应对巨大压力。我们每个人都有不同的需求和界限（麦格隆教授认为"不是每个人都缺乏接触；我真的不喜欢被拥抱，而这让我可怜的妻子抓狂"），但完全缺乏接触，尤其是在情绪激动的时候，则违背了人类自不会说话的婴儿时期就刻在遗传基因里的需求。

7 福托普卢教授表示："触觉是一种调节器，可以调节压力、疼痛对身体、情绪的影响。我们在研究中发现，缺乏肢体接触会加重焦虑。在压力较大的时期——比如失业或丧亲之痛——与他人更多的肢体接触有助于人们更好地应对压力，尤其能够缓解（压力荷尔蒙）皮质醇的影响。"即使人们习惯了更少的肢体接触，一段时间后这种需求也会被人体感知到，这种情况有时被称为"皮肤饥饿"或"触摸饥饿"。

8 虽然我能体会到家有孩子的朋友们对我描述的那种令人筋疲力尽的单调（当然我明白这山望着那山高的道理），但我还是强烈地感觉到缺乏属于某个群体的归属感。来自爱丁堡的教师克莱尔·伯克（Claire Birke）也有同感，她说："我37岁了，大多数朋友都和伴侣或孩子住在一起，在我的生活中，从未如此强烈察觉到自己的单身状态，也从未如此意识到我缺乏亲密的身体接触。"

9 1997年至2017年间，英国独立生活的人数增加了16%，达到770万。社交气泡圈所带来的少量社交活动也令人感到了极大的抚慰。史密斯和一对住在一起的情侣就属于同一个"社交气泡"，她认为这有助于改善其情绪。但未来日子还长，她的朋友们"无法被真实地触碰到"。

10 史密斯说："我意识到我频繁地不假思索地触摸别人，我觉得自己把所有这些情感都藏在了我的身体里，无处流露。"

11 在高压力状态下，如果没有人拥抱我们，我们的身体几乎无法控制自身的情绪。福托普卢教授认为："许多研究支持这样一种理论，即触摸给大脑一个信号，大脑可以调配资源应对压力，因为（大脑知道）有其他人分担最糟糕的结果。这能够让身体放松下来，以某种方式恢复压力阈值，只要你愿意这么做。”但触觉并不是一种单一的感觉。我们皮肤的面积达两平方米，其中充满了识别温度、质地和瘙痒等的神经纤维。其中一组纤维的存在正是为了记录温柔的抚摸感，即 CT 触觉传入纤维（CTs）。自 1995 年这一纤维在人类身上被发现以来，麦格隆一直在研究它。“在所有群居哺乳动物的皮肤中，这些神经元将缓慢的电信号传输到大脑的情绪处理部分。它们在发展社会脑和人承受压力的能力方面发挥着关键作用。”

12 全身 CT 触觉传入纤维密度最高的部位是我们不能自己“梳理”的部位，比如肩膀和背部。麦格隆教授表示：“如果你喜欢背部按摩，那是因为那里有更多的 CT 触觉传入纤维。对这些神经元的刺激会释放催产素和多巴胺，并对调节情绪的皮质醇水平产生直接影响。”2017 年，福托普卢教授的团队发表了一项研究，表明即使是陌生人温和、缓慢的抚摸也能减少社会排斥感。但在我们的正常生活中，我们不会一直聚在一起互相抚摸。麦格隆说：“不，你不需要整天都用那种触碰。我们只需要间断性地进行这种温柔的抚摸。”

13 在这个缺乏触摸的时代，没有一种行为能真正替代其他人类可带来的感觉，但我们有办法安慰自己。福托普卢教授的实验室很快将发表一项在新冠大流行期间进行的研究，该研究建立在这样一个理论的基础上，即我们认为自己能够感受到他人的痛苦，我们也或许能够以间接的方式体验触摸。研究人员发现，看到触摸（例如在电视或电影中），尤其是社交性的、实际发生的触摸或抚摸宠物，可以让我们感受到触摸的一些好处。福托普卢教授说：“这被称为‘触摸替代’，大脑以多种方式编码多感官体验。我们也可以通过‘看到’他人的痛苦和快乐来‘感觉’他们。这不是永久或完全的替代品，只是部分替代品。”

14 类似厚重毯子之类的产品会有助于“触摸替代”。史密斯说，把一个厚毯子放在她的胸部和肩膀上会让她感觉“平静多了”——这也许是出于刺激 CT 触觉传入纤维的本能需要。与动物的互动也有类似效果。“邻居家的猫大部分时间都和我住在一起，猫猫坐在我胸前发出咕噜咕噜的声音，这真的很治愈。”

15 这引起了我的共鸣：在过去的 12 个月里，我的手一直摸着我家狗狗的温暖背部，这是对我而言在那段日子里最接地气、具体可感的事物。我知道这感觉很好，但为什么呢？麦格隆说：“当你抚摸狗狗时，身体内一些系统会得以激活，产生和狗狗抚摸你类似的效果。”

16 对触摸的渴望是原始需求没有得到满足的信号。但进化给了人类适应的能力。与我交谈过的每一位科学家都希望，一旦我们再次相聚，我们将做出迅速的调整。邓巴说：“每个人的情况不同，可能取决于人们独处的时间长短，还可能会有一段别扭和重新适应的时期。但我们已经进化到能够适应这些调整了。”

图书在版编目（CIP）数据

跨文化思辨阅读教程. 生活篇 / 袁风识主编. —北京：中国人民大学出版社，2023.7
全人教育英语专业本科教材系列 / 文旭总主编
ISBN 978-7-300-31934-6

Ⅰ. ①跨…　Ⅱ. ①袁…　Ⅲ. ①英语—阅读教学—高等学校—教材　Ⅳ. ①H319.37

中国国家版本馆 CIP 数据核字（2023）第 130134 号

全人教育英语专业本科教材系列
总顾问　刘润清
总主编　文　旭
跨文化思辨阅读教程（生活篇）
主　编　袁风识
副主编　秦小雅　李银美
编　者　张翼鸿　高　黎　王亚非
杨仁瑛　赵宏伟　张慧馨
张　潇　徐召华
Kuawenhua Sibian Yuedu Jiaocheng (Shenghuo Pian)

出版发行	中国人民大学出版社		
社　址	北京中关村大街 31 号	邮政编码	100080
电　话	010-62511242（总编室）		010-62511770（质管部）
	010-82501766（邮购部）		010-62514148（门市部）
	010-62515195（发行公司）		010-62515275（盗版举报）
网　址	http:// www. crup. com. cn		
经　销	新华书店		
印　刷	北京密兴印刷有限公司		
开　本	889 mm × 1194 mm　1/16	版　次	2023 年 7 月第 1 版
印　张	12	印　次	2023 年 7 月第 1 次印刷
字　数	258 000	定　价	49.00 元

中国人民大学出版社读者信息反馈表

尊敬的读者：

感谢您购买和使用中国人民大学出版社的 ______________________ 一书，我们希望通过这张小小的反馈卡来获得您更多的建议和意见，以改进我们的工作，加强我们双方的沟通和联系。我们期待着能为更多的读者提供更多的好书。

请您填妥下表后，寄回或传真回复我们，对您的支持我们不胜感激！

1. 您是从何种途径得知本书的：

□书店　□网上　□报纸杂志　□朋友推荐

2. 您为什么决定购买本书：

□工作需要　□学习参考　□对本书主题感兴趣　□随便翻翻

3. 您对本书内容的评价是：

□很好　□好　□一般　□差　□很差

4. 您在阅读本书的过程中有没有发现明显的专业及编校错误，如果有，它们是：

____

____

____

5. 您对哪些专业的图书信息比较感兴趣：

____

____

____

6. 如果方便，请提供您的个人信息，以便于我们和您联系（您的个人资料我们将严格保密）：

您供职的单位：______________________________________

您教授的课程（教师填写）：__________________________

您的通信地址：______________________________________

您的电子邮箱：______________________________________

请联系我们：黄婷　程子殊　王新文　王琼　鞠方安

电话：010-62512737，62513265，62515580，62515573，62515576

传真：010-62514961

E-mail：huangt@crup.com.cn　chengzsh@crup.com.cn　wangxw@crup.com.cn　crup_wy@163.com　jufa@crup.com.cn

通信地址：北京市海淀区中关村大街甲59号文化大厦15层　邮编：100872

中国人民大学出版社